NEXT
GENERATION LEADER

NEXT

GENERATION

LEADER

FIVE ESSENTIALS FOR THOSE
WHO WILL SHAPE THE FUTURE

ANDY STANLEY

Multnomah®Publishers *Sisters, Oregon*

THE NEXT GENERATION LEADER

published by Multnomah Publishers, Inc.

© 2003 by Andy Stanley

International Standard Book Number: 1-59052-539-6

Unless otherwise indicated, Scripture quotations are from:
New American Standard Bible© 1960, 1977, 1995
by the Lockman Foundation. Used by permission.

Other Scripture quotations are from:
The Holy Bible, New International Version (NIV) © 1973, 1984 by
International Bible Society, used by permission of
Zondervan Publishing House

Multnomah is a trademark of Multnomah Publishers, Inc.,
and is registered in the U.S. Patent and Trademark Office.
The colophon is a trademark of Multnomah Publishers, Inc.

Printed in the United States of America

For information:
MULTNOMAH PUBLISHERS, INC.
601 N LARCH STREET
SISTERS, OREGON 97759

Library of Congress Cataloging-in-Publication Data

Stanley, Andy.
    The next generation leader / Andy Stanley.
            p. cm.
Includes bibliographical references.

        ISBN 1-59052-046-7 (hardback)
        ISBN 1-59052-232-X

    1. Christian leadership. I. Title.

BV652.1 .S69 2003

253--dc21   2002014699

07 08 09 10—14 13 12 11

For my children,

ANDREW, GARRETT, AND ALLIE.

CONTENTS

INTRODUCTION

The more you know about leadership, the faster you grow as a leader and the farther you are able to go as a leader. Learning from the experiences of others enables you to go farther, faster. It is that simple truth that inspired me to write *Next Generation Leader*.

As the pastor of a church with a median age of thirty, I find myself surrounded by next generation leaders—men and women who have the potential to shape their generation. They are eager to learn. They are committed to personal growth. And given the chance, they will attempt things that my generation only dreamed about.

The success of North Point Community Church has provided me a window of opportunity. For the time being, a segment of this remarkable group of men and women is interested in what I have to say about leadership. So I consider it my responsibility to hand off what I have learned while I have the chance.

If much will be required from those to whom much has been given, then much will be required of me. For I have been given much in the way of example, opportunity, and training.

I grew up in the shadow of my father, Charles Stanley, a gifted communicator and accomplished leader. Yet in spite of his professional responsibilities he never missed a basketball game or failed to carve out time for extensive summer vacations. I was nurtured by a mom who saw it as her mission to prepare me to leave the nest with the security and skills necessary to thrive in this unpredictable world.

By the time I was fourteen my parents had pretty much quit making decisions for me and thereby forced me to decide for myself and live with the consequences of my decisions. I never had a curfew. My dad asked me when I planned to be home, and that's when I headed home. To my knowledge, they never waited up.

I was given lots of freedom. I was also given the full measure of responsibility that went along with that freedom. When I got my first speeding ticket—a whopping two weeks after I'd received my license—my dad's only comment was, "Better slow down." No lectures. No suspended driving privileges. He figured the fine was punishment enough.

I was no angel. In many respects I was a typical preacher's kid. But my wise parents gave me very little to rebel against. Instead they loaded me up with what, looking back, appears to be an almost naïve amount of trust.

In hindsight, I can see that my parents raised me to lead. In terms of actual practice and principles, more was caught than taught. I don't remember a single conversation that centered on the subject of leadership. But through the vision they cast and the opportunities they provided, I was given an incredible head start as a leader.

For that reason, I am convinced that it is my responsibility to pass on what I know about leadership to the generation coming along behind me. So it has been the habit of my life to carve out time for the next generation, the capable men and women who will eventually catch, pass, and replace me.

When I was in college, that next generation was high school students. When I was in graduate school, it was undergrads. When I landed my first real job, I invested in young men headed into ministry. In addition, I spent ten years meeting with small groups of high school seniors, pouring into their cups all I could from my own.

This has been my lifestyle. For many of those who were part of my groups, it has become their lifestyle as well. A handful are now in full-time ministry. One serves as the worship leader at our church. Another is now my stockbroker. Some fly airplanes; some have their own companies; most are married, with children. A few have dropped off the map.

I approach this task of handing off what I have learned with the full knowledge that in the days to come the next generation's gifts to this world will certainly eclipse whatever I have had to offer. But, then, that's the point. In leadership, *success* is *succession*. If someone coming along behind me is not able to take what I have offered and build on it, then I have failed in my responsibility to the next generation.

I began this project with a series of questions:

1. What are the leadership principles I wish someone had shared with me when I was a young leader?
2. What do I know now that I wish I had known then?
3. Of all that *could* be said about leadership, what must be conveyed to next generation leaders?

I identified five concepts that serve as the outline of this book. These represent what I believe to be the irreducible minimum, the essentials for next generation leaders:

1. COMPETENCE

Leaders must channel their energies toward those arenas of leadership in which they are most likely to excel.

2. COURAGE

The leader of an enterprise isn't always the smartest or most creative person on the team. He isn't necessarily the first to identify an opportunity. The leader is the one who has the courage to initiate, to set things in motion, to move ahead.

3. CLARITY

Uncertain times require clear directives from those in leadership. Yet the temptation for young leaders is to allow uncertainty to *leave them paralyzed*. A next generation leader must learn to be clear even when he is not certain.

4. COACHING

You may be good. You may even be better than everyone else. But without a coach you will never be as good as you could be.

5. CHARACTER

You can lead without character, but you won't be a leader worth following. Character provides next generation leaders with the moral authority necessary to bring together the people and resources needed to further an enterprise.

If God has gifted you to lead, then lead you will. There's no stopping you. More than likely, people have already recognized your gift and are lining up to follow you. My passion is to help equip you to become a leader whose life is marked by qualities that ensure a no-regrets experience for those who choose to follow; a leader who leaves this world in better shape than he found it.

You think that is a stretch?

Think about it: Individuals from your generation will surface as leaders in every field—business, art, politics, economics, math, technology, medicine, religion. Those men and women will shape the future during your lifetime. Nobody knows who they are. You might as well throw your hat into the ring by leveraging your gifts and opportunities for all they're worth. Embracing these five essentials will enable you to do just that.

So let's begin.

COMPETENCE

DO LESS, ACCOMPLISH MORE

Chapter One

YOU ARE DOING TOO MUCH!

The secret of concentration is elimination.

[Dr. Howard Hendricks]

It is both natural and necessary for young leaders to try to prove themselves by doing everything themselves. It is natural because, as a leader, you want to set the pace even as you demonstrate that nothing is beneath you. It is necessary because most of the time nobody is around to help. But what may initially be natural and necessary will ultimately limit your effectiveness.

Perhaps the two best-kept secrets of leadership are these:

1. The less you do, the more you accomplish.

2. The less you do, the more you enable others to accomplish.

As a young leader, my biggest mistake was allowing my time to be eaten up with things outside my core competencies. I devoted an inordinate amount of my first seven years in ministry to things I was not good at—things I would *never* be good at. At the same time, I invested little energy in developing my strengths.

I am a good communicator. I am not a good manager.

I am a good visioncaster. I am not good at follow-up. I know how to prepare a message. I am not good at planning an event.

And yet early on I did nothing to hone my communication skills. Instead, I spent a great deal of time trying to become a better manager and a better event planner. When it came to communication, I would often wing it because the time I should have used to prepare talks had been consumed by other things. And this was the one area in which I *could* wing it.

The problem was that somewhere along the way I had bought into the myth that a good leader has to be good at everything. So I operated under the assumption that I had to upgrade my weaknesses into strengths. After all, who would follow a leader who wasn't well-rounded?

After graduate school I went to work for my dad. As a minister to students my primary responsibilities revolved around developing a strategy for involving junior high and high school students in the life of the church.

The fact that this was my first job opportunity after grad school, combined with the reality that I was working for my dad, sent me into the workforce determined to succeed. I felt the need to prove myself by working harder than everyone else around me. I came in early and went home late. I was in constant motion.

But I did not work smart. The majority of my time was devoted to tasks I was not good at. I was eight years into my career before I realized that my real value to our organization lay within the context of my giftedness, not the number of hours I worked.

From that point forward I began looking for ways to

redefine my job description according to what I was good at, rather than simply what I was willing to do. I discovered that there were some balls I had no business juggling. When I finally mustered the courage to let 'em fall to the floor and roll over in the corner, I began to excel in juggling the two or three balls I was created to keep in the air in the first place.

My success attracted others who were committed to the same cause. While we shared the same passion for students, our skill-sets were different. It wasn't long before they began picking up the stray balls I had let fall. The responsibilities I was reluctant to relinquish turned out to be opportunities for others. The very activities that drained me fueled other team members.

Consequently, I began to do more communicating and less event planning. I learned how to spend the majority of my time at the thirty-thousand-foot level while remaining accessible to team members who were closer to the action. I spent more time strategizing and less time problem solving. I became far more proactive about what I allowed on my calendar. I became more mission-driven rather than need-driven, and now I want to give you that same vision as it relates to your core competencies:

ONLY DO WHAT ONLY YOU CAN DO.

This might seem unrealistic from where you sit today. You might even laugh out loud. But once you get past the seeming improbability of this axiom, write it down and work toward it.

What are the two or three things that you and only you are responsible for? What, specifically, have you been hired to do? What is "success" for the person in your position?

Now let's slice it even thinner. Of the two or three things that define success for you, which of those are in line with your giftedness? Of the tasks you have been assigned to do, which of them are you specifically gifted to do?

That is where you must focus your energies. That is your sweet spot. That is where you will excel. Within that narrowed context you will add the most value to your organization. Success within that sphere has the potential to make you indispensable to your employer.

Best of all, you will enjoy what you do.

"Impossible!" you say. "I can't afford to focus my energies on only a percentage of my overall responsibilities!"

Maybe not yet. But you owe it to yourself to identify the areas in which you have the highest probability for success. You owe it to your employer to identify the areas in which you could add the most value to your organization. You can't aim for a target until you have identified it. We're talking about a mind-set here, a perspective, a way of thinking. This is a vision. This is something you must work toward to maximize your potential as a leader.

During the 2001 baseball season, Greg Maddux of the Atlanta Braves had a batting average of .253—average by professional standards. Yet he is one of the most highly sought-after players in the National Baseball League. Why? Because in his role as pitcher, he struck out 173 batters the previous year. His skill with a bat is not what makes him an indispensable part of the lineup. His ninety-mile-an-hour fastball does.

Should he spend more time working on his hitting? Maybe—but certainly not at the expense of his pitching.

Identify the areas in which you are most likely to add unique value to your organization—something no one else can match—then leverage your skills to their absolute max. That's what your employer expected when he put you on the payroll! More importantly, leveraging yourself generates the greatest and most satisfying return on your God-given abilities.

The moment a leader steps away from his core competencies, his effectiveness as a leader diminishes. Worse, the effectiveness of every other leader in the organization suffers too. In time, a leader who is not leading from the right "zone" will create an unfavorable environment for other leaders.

Let me explain. Using John Maxwell's one-to-ten leadership scale, score yourself as a leader[1]. If you are an exceptional leader, give yourself an eight or a nine. If you consider yourself an average leader, give yourself a five or a six. For the sake of illustration, let's say that when you're at the top of your game you are a seven.

Maxwell argues that at a seven, you will attract followers who are fives and sixes. If you were a nine, you would attract sevens and eights. In other words, leaders attract other leaders whose skills come close to matching but rarely surpass their own.

Perhaps you've known the frustration of working for someone whose leadership skills were inferior to yours. It probably wasn't long before you were looking for another place to work. On the other hand, you might know the thrill of working for leaders whose leadership skills were superior to yours.

Such environments probably brought out the best in you.

Now, back to my point. Assuming you are a seven, you will be at your best when you are in your zone—that is, when you are devoting your time to the things you are naturally gifted to do. That's when you operate as a seven. And as a seven, you will attract fives and sixes. And, if you are secure, other sevens.

Furthermore, you may have seven potential, but outside your core competencies you will lead like a six. If you continue in that mode, you will lose the devotion and possibly the respect of the other sixes around you. In time, you will dumb down the leadership level of your entire organization—everybody suffers.

Like most good principles, this one is somewhat intuitive. It makes sense. Yet many a leader has leaned his shoulder into the wind and forged ahead, determined to do it all and do it all well. In fact, you may get into a head-versus-heart battle of your own as you reflect on the implications of this idea. No doubt your heart leaps with excitement at the thought of concentrating on the areas in which you naturally excel. Intuitively you know that's the way to go. But your head says, "Wait a minute—it can't be that simple!"

After challenging hundreds of leaders to play to their strengths, I have identified five primary obstacles to a leader adopting this way of thinking.

1. THE QUEST FOR BALANCE

The first thing that sometimes keeps next generation leaders from playing to their strengths is that the idea of being a balanced or well-rounded leader looks good on paper and sounds compelling coming from behind a lectern, but in reality, it is an unworthy endeavor. Read the biographies of the achievers in any arena of life. You will find over and over that these were not "well-rounded" leaders. They were men and women of *focus*.

We should strive for balance organizationally, but it is not realistic to strive for balance within the sphere of our personal leadership abilities. Striving for balance forces a leader to invest time and energy in aspects of leadership where he will never excel. When the point person in an organization strives for balance, he potentially robs other leaders of an opportunity to perform at the top of their game.

My current context for leadership is the local church. Like most churches, ours has a component that focuses exclusively on high school students. The person who tackles that responsibility is usually someone who excels in leading people from the platform. Student pastors are often animated, pied-piper individuals.

The fellow who leads that charge at North Point is not. Kevin Ragsdale is a great example of a singularly focused, highly effective leader. Yet Kevin's strength is administration. By his own admission, Kevin is not a great platform personality. Rather than waste his time trying to become proficient in an area where he may never excel, Kevin has trained and mentored a group of individuals who are gifted communicators and visioncasters.

In other words, Kevin is not well-rounded in his leadership ability, but his organization is well-rounded. He focuses on what he is gifted in and empowers others to do the same. Consequently, anyone who walks into our student environments will be wowed by the excellence of communication, but equally impressed by the quality of the programming and the organization that supports it.

When a leader attempts to become well-rounded, he brings down the average of the organization's leadership quotient—which brings down the level of the leaders around him. Don't strive to be a well-rounded leader. Instead, discover your zone and stay there. Then delegate everything else.

2. FAILURE TO DISTINGUISH BETWEEN AUTHORITY AND COMPETENCE

The second reason leaders don't always play to their strengths is that they have yet to distinguish between authority and competency. Every leader has authority over arenas in which he has little or no competence. When we exert our authority in an area where we lack competence, we can derail projects and demotivate those who have the skills we lack.

On any given Sunday morning I have the authority to walk into our video control room and start barking out orders. The fact that I don't know the first thing about what's going on in there does not diminish my authority. Eventually the crew would do what I asked them to do. But the production would suffer horribly. If I were to do that Sunday after Sunday, our best and brightest volunteers would leave. Eventually our paid staff would start looking for something else to do as well.

There is no need to become an expert in, or even to understand, every component of your organization. When you try to exercise authority within a department that is outside your core competencies, you will hinder everything and everyone under your watch. If you fail to distinguish between authority and competence, you will exert your influence in ways that damage projects and people.

To put it bluntly, there are things you are responsible for that you should keep your nose out of.

3. INABILITY TO DISTINGUISH BETWEEN COMPETENCIES AND NONCOMPETENCIES

Leaders who are successful in one arena often assume competency in arenas where in fact they have none. As a result, they miss opportunities to leverage their strengths. As we will discuss later, success is an intoxicant, and intoxicated people seldom have a firm grasp on reality. Successful leaders tend to assume that their core competencies are broader than they actually are.

Worse, the more successful an individual is, the less likely it is that anyone will bring this unpleasant fact to his attention. Consequently, a leader considered an expert in one area is often treated as an expert in others as well.

Leaders who are not in touch with their own weaknesses feel that they are as good as anybody else in their organization at anything that pertains to leadership. Many have even bought into the false notion that great leaders have no weaknesses. In their minds, to admit weakness is to diminish their effectiveness. Such leaders tend to hide their weaknesses, assuming they ever discover them.

Recently I received a call from a board member of an international organization. He wanted my advice about how to handle a conflict between the board and the founder of the organization, who was serving as president. The president was a gifted visioncaster who had raised a great deal of capital for the company. In fact, the success of this organization was due in large part to his ability to communicate effectively to a wide range of audiences.

But he was not a particularly great businessman. The board wanted to hire a top-notch CFO, but the president believed he could continue to oversee that aspect of the organization in his role as president. In recent days the president had made decisions that raised questions about his business savvy. It was apparent to everyone except him that he needed to stay out of the business side and focus his attention on what made him and the company successful to begin with. His problem was not IQ; it was insight. He just didn't get it.

In general, an inability to own up to personal shortcomings is often rooted in some sort of insecurity. This can be easy to see in others but next to impossible to see in ourselves. It takes a certain amount of personal security to admit weakness.

And the truth is that admitting a weakness is a sign of strength. Acknowledging weakness doesn't make a leader less effective. On the contrary, in most cases it is simply a way of expressing that he understands what everyone else has known for some time. When you acknowledge your weaknesses to the rest of your team, it is never new information.

4. GUILT

Some leaders don't play only to their strengths because they feel guilty delegating their weaknesses.

This is where I struggle. I assume everybody hates to do the things I hate to do. For years I felt guilty delegating responsibilities that I really didn't want to get involved with in the first place. It took me a while to realize that the leaders around me were energized by the very things that drained the life out of me.

As I mentioned earlier, planning and producing events is not one of my strengths. Planning just about anything is terribly stressful to me. Early in my career I would apologetically delegate event planning, incorrectly assuming that everyone dreaded this type of thing as much as I did. Yet I assumed I was doing everybody a favor when I took responsibility for planning and producing events.

Fortunately for our entire organization, I discovered that I was surrounded by leaders whose adrenal glands went into overdrive at the prospect of planning an event. Not only were they good at it; they enjoyed it! I have to laugh when I think about how diplomatic my leadership team was as they pried my hands from certain events.

Remember, everybody in your organization benefits when you delegate responsibilities that fall outside your core competency. Thoughtful delegation will allow someone else in your organization to shine. Your weakness is someone's opportunity.

5. UNWILLINGNESS TO DEVELOP OTHER LEADERS

There is some truth to the adage "If you want it done right, do it yourself." Sometimes it really is easier and less time-consuming to do things yourself than to train someone else. But leadership is not always about getting things done "right." Leadership is about getting things done through other people. Leaders miss opportunities to play to their strengths because they haven't figured out that great leaders work through other leaders, who work through others. Leadership is about multiplying your efforts, which automatically multiplies your results.

As one author put it:

> We accomplish all that we do through delegation—
> either to time or to other people…. Transferring
> responsibility to other skilled and trained people
> enables you to give your energies to other high-
> leverage activities. Delegation means growth, both
> for individuals and for organizations.[2]

Every once in a while I will hear someone in leadership complain about the performance or competency of the people around him. When a leader can't find someone to hand things off to, it is time for him to look in the mirror. We must never forget that the people who follow us are exactly where we have led them. If there is no one to whom we can delegate, it is our own fault.

Many examples in history underscore the centrality of this catalytic leadership principle. Each illustrates the fact that you never know what hangs in the balance of a decision to play to your strengths.

Oddly enough, it was the prudent application of this principle that enabled the fledgling first-century church to consolidate its gains and capitalize on its explosive growth, without losing focus or momentum.

Chapter Two

DOING THE RIGHT THINGS

We have different gifts, according to the
grace given us. If a man's gift is...leadership,
let him govern diligently.

[Romans 12:6, 8, NIV]

Leaders in the first-century church had no model to follow and no traditions from which to draw. Consequently, they had no choice but to develop the structure of the church as they went along. As you might expect, the primary leadership responsibilities fell to the handful of men who had spent the most time with Jesus. That was fine in the early days. But as the church grew, it became impossible for the apostles to keep all the plates spinning. This growing tension created the need for broader leadership in the early church.

In those days when the number of disciples was increasing, the Grecian Jews among them complained against the Hebraic Jews because their widows were being overlooked in the daily distribution of food. So the Twelve gathered all the disciples together and said, "It would not be right for us to neglect the ministry of the word of God in order to wait on tables. Brothers, choose seven men from among you who are known to be full of the Spirit and wisdom. We will turn this responsibility over to them and will give our attention to prayer and the ministry of the word."

This proposal pleased the whole group. They chose Stephen, a man full of faith and of the Holy Spirit; also Philip, Procorus, Nicanor, Timon, Parmenas, and Nicolas from Antioch, a convert to Judaism. They presented these men to the apostles, who prayed and laid their hands on them.

So the word of God spread. The number of disciples in Jerusalem increased rapidly, and a large number of priests became obedient to the faith. (Acts 6:1–7, NIV).

It's hard to imagine the apostle Peter as a waiter. But as the church grew, he and the other eleven apostles found themselves in the food service business. The widows in the first-century church had to be cared for.[3] Somebody had to do it. And nothing was beneath these men.

After all, these were the fellows who had watched in dismay as Jesus stooped to wash their feet. They knew all about servant leadership. They had learned from the Master Servant Himself. So, if the widows needed to be fed, why not go ahead and feed them?

But eventually the job outgrew them. More and more of their time was being consumed by administrative activities. And apparently administration wasn't something they were exceptionally good at, because before long it appeared that they were being partial to the Hebraic Jews in the daily distribution of food.[4]

At some point they realized things had to change. The

mission of the church was at risk. The main thing was no longer *their* main thing. So they did what any good church would do: They called a meeting.

Pay close attention to their opening statement: "It would not be right for us to neglect the ministry of the word of God in order to wait on tables" (v. 2). That's pretty strong. In other words, "We would be doing the wrong thing to continue caring for the widows." I just hope there weren't any widows at the meeting!

The apostles came to terms early on with the notion that they had to do what only they could do. They were the only men on the planet who were equipped to recommunicate the teachings of Christ. Their unique experiences and unlimited access to the Master had positioned them as the sole bearers of the most important message in the world.

Given that imperative, they had no business waiting on tables. To do so would have had a negative impact on the momentum and focus of the church. It was time to delegate both responsibility and authority so they could continue doing the two things they were best equipped to do: teach and pray.

Unlike the modern church, they did not ask for volunteers. They chose seven men who were equipped to handle the task. They were not shirking their responsibility by doing this. On the contrary, they were choosing in such a way as to ensure that the job would be done better than before.

And the result? "So the word of God spread. The number of disciples in Jerusalem increased rapidly, and a large number of priests became obedient to the faith" (Acts 6:7, NIV).

Three things happened as a result of this seemingly insignificant decision:

1. The word of God spread.

2. The number of disciples in Jerusalem increased rapidly.

3. Key influencers in the city were converted.

In short, they stayed on task. And while the apostles remained in the spotlight, seven other men worked behind the scenes to make sure the money and food were handled responsibly.

Was the task of these seven newcomers any less "spiritual" than that of the apostles? No. Was their responsibility any less crucial to the success of the church? Of course not. Both groups were indispensable to the progress of the gospel. But it wasn't until they were positioned correctly that their impact was fully felt.

Something else happened as a result of the apostles' decision to delegate the distribution of food. Two new leaders surfaced: Stephen and Philip. Stephen went on to become a powerful public witness and eventually the first post-Pentecost martyr. Philip became a traveling evangelist. His ministry resulted in the conversion of many outside the region of Jerusalem, where the majority of the apostles continued to teach.[5] Both of these men were given their first opportunities in ministry as a result of the apostles' decision to do what only they could do.

None of the Twelve had any idea what hung in the balance of their decision to give up waiting tables. What they did know was that it would not be right for them to "neglect the ministry of the word." Imagine what might have happened if these leaders had continued waiting tables and hadn't delegated the responsibility of disseminating food.

The same principle is true for you. Like the apostles, you have no idea what hangs in the balance of your decision to play to your strengths and delegate your weaknesses. As a leader, gifted by God to do a few things well, it is not right for you to attempt to do everything.

> Upgrade your performance by playing to your strengths and delegating your weaknesses. This one decision will do more to enhance your productivity than anything else you do as a leader.

I once heard John Maxwell say, "You are most valuable where you add the most value." It is vital to the health and success of our organizations that we as leaders discover that task, that narrow arena of responsibility where we add the most value. And once we find it, it's even more vital that we stay there.

In a letter to seminary alumni, Dr. Howard Hendricks underscored the importance of this principle:

> If anything has kept me on track all these years, it's being skewered to this principle of central focus. There are many things I can do, but I have to narrow it down to the one thing I *must* do. The secret of concentration is elimination. (emphasis added)

As you evaluate your current leadership environment and responsibilities, what do you see that needs to be eliminated? What needs to be delegated? What would it "not be right" for you to continue doing?

Chapter Three

FINDING YOUR GROOVE

Devoting a little of yourself to
everything means committing a great deal of
yourself to nothing.

There is no necessary correlation between how busy
you are and how productive you are. Being busy isn't the
same as being productive.

Chances are, you are as busy now as you have ever been.
But does that mean you are being as productive as you could
possibly be? Of course not. Full schedules rarely equal maximum productivity. In fact, I would argue that the opposite
is true. The most productive people I know seem to have
more, not less, discretionary time than the average person.
They control their schedules rather than allowing their
schedules to control them.

Observation and analysis confirm that 20 percent of our
efforts result in 80 percent of our effectiveness. Richard
Koch, in his groundbreaking work *The 80/20 Principle,* docu-
ments this important relationship:

The 80/20 Principle asserts that a minority of causes,
inputs, or effort usually lead to a majority of the

results, outputs, or rewards. Taken literally, this means that, for example, 80 percent of what you achieve in your job comes from 20 percent of the time spent. Thus for all practical purposes, four-fifths of the effort—a dominant part of it—is largely irrelevant.[6]

If Koch is right, it is imperative that we discover the 20 percent of what we do that generates the 80 percent of our productivity. Having discovered it, we must focus more of our time and energy on those activities. Therein lies the key to maximum impact as a leader.

Several years ago I concluded that 80 percent of my professional productivity flowed from three activities:

■ Corporate visioncasting

■ Corporate communication

■ Leadership development

These were the three things that made me most valuable to my organization. My competence in these areas defines my success as a pastor. As the senior pastor these are the things that only I can do.

With that in mind, I sat down with my assistant, Diane Grant, and began rearranging and reprioritizing my schedule around these three things. I almost doubled the time set aside for sermon preparation and evaluation. I committed an entire day each week to staff development. And I increased the percentage of Sunday morning platform time given to visioncasting. Over 80 percent of my time is now focused on the three things that only I can do.

In my line of work, the majority of my success hinges

on a weekly forty-minute presentation referred to in most circles as a sermon. It doesn't matter how many hours I work. For the most part, my success hinges on whether or not I can deliver the goods on Sunday morning. A sixty-hour workweek will not compensate for a poorly delivered sermon. People don't show up on Sunday morning because I am a good pastor (leader, shepherd, counselor). Ironically, my pastoring skills have almost nothing to do with my success as a pastor! In my world, it is my communication skills that make the difference. So that is where I focus my time.

To use Koch's paradigm, you must commit more of your time to the 20 percent activities. Doing so will increase your productivity and your value to your organization. The primary reason we do too much is that we have never taken the time to discover that portion of what we do that makes the biggest difference.

The following questions are designed to help you discover your core competencies. Take a few minutes to do some personal evaluation. You might find it helpful to take a few notes as you work through this list.

1. What do you do that is almost effortless from your perspective but seems like a daunting task to others?

2. In what arenas do people consider you the "go-to" person?

3. What do you enjoy about your current job?

4. What do you wish you could delegate?

5. What do you do that elicits the most praise and recognition from others?

6. What environments do you look forward to working in?

7. What environments do you avoid?

8. What kind of advice do people seek from you?

9. If you could focus more of your time and attention on one or two aspects of your job, what would they be?

Self-evaluation is a necessary step in discovering your core competencies. But it is not enough. No one is completely objective about himself. For that reason, you would be wise to involve other people in this process. Choose two or three people who know you well and who employ others, and ask them to answer these questions about you:

1. If I came to work for you for free…

   ■ where in your organization would I add the most value?

   ■ where would you want me to focus my attention?

   ■ where would I stand the most chance of success?

   ■ what area or areas would you see to it that I avoid?

2. In my current work environment, where do you see misalignment between my core competencies and my responsibilities?

3. If you had an opportunity to advise my boss on how to better utilize me, what would your advice be?

4. Are you aware of areas in my life where there is misalignment between my passion and my competency?[7]

A third project you can do to help you surface your real strengths is to develop two job descriptions for yourself. Your first one should reflect current reality. The second one, your ideal job description.

Assume for the moment that you are going to work for your current employer for the next two years. How would you adjust your current job description to position you to add greater value to the organization? How could your employer better use you? Which of your gifts are not currently being utilized to their fullest?

Once you have completed this project, present it to your boss. His response will tell you a great deal about your future with that organization. If your supervisor is wise, he will view your initiative as a potential opportunity to realign things to increase productivity. Essentially, you have put time and effort into trying to improve his productivity as well as your own. If your boss feels threatened by your proposal, that is an indication that he has probably put personal interests ahead of corporate interests. If that's the case, you may want to start looking around for another environment in which to invest your talents.

If your employer is going to pay you anyway, he might as well squeeze the most value out of you he can. Nobody benefits from organizational misalignment. Misalignment is expensive. It results in unnecessary wear and tear, personally and corporately.

I have made it a habit to ask our top people these questions: "What do you want to do? How can I help you find greater satisfaction within this organization? Where are your skills not being put to good use? How can I help you focus more of your time and energy on the thing(s) that tap your core competencies as well as add value to this organization?"

Because of my relationship with our leadership team, I feel comfortable talking to them about what they are interested in professionally beyond the walls of North Point Community Church. I am surrounded by leaders who could launch off in any number of directions and be successful. If they feel the need to invest their talents somewhere else, I don't want them to keep that from me because of fear or guilt. I want them to feel like they can count on me to support them in any new enterprise they feel led to pursue.

In one of my monthly leadership talks with our staff, I challenged them to revise their job descriptions and present them to their supervisors. The response was overwhelming. What I wasn't smart enough to anticipate was that I was giving our staff permission to express some things they had been thinking about but were not sure how well they would be received.

We know when we are misemployed. We know when our talents and efforts are being misappropriated. What we don't know is how open our supervisors are to hearing about it. As a result of this assignment we made some significant changes that brought about better alignment for the entire staff. Furthermore, we stumbled upon a new tool by which to uncover what our people were thinking and feeling.

Now, if you are an employer, you may be thinking, *Isn't that kind of dangerous? Aren't you afraid of losing your best people? Aren't you concerned about the stability and future success of your organization?* The answer to all three is *no*. First of all, they aren't "your" people. Second, it is not "your" organization. Besides, I tell 'em all the time that if they leave, I'm going with them! Eventually they are all leaving anyway. I've simply decided that it is better to launch people than lose them.

In addition to a job description designed around your *current* employment, develop what you would consider to be the *ultimate* job description. This is for your eyes only. The goal of this exercise is to help you identify the niche in which you would feel most productive and consequently most successful. Dream a little.

What if you could do anything and work anywhere? What would you do? Where would you do it? Who would you work with? Go ahead; write it down. Sure, it may seem unrealistic from where you sit today. But visions always seem unrealistic when they are first hatched. This is a vision, not a plan.

Organize the vision for your dream job around two things: environment and responsibilities.

1. In light of your strengths, weaknesses, gifts, and passions, describe the optimal working environment.

    ■ What kind of people would you enjoy working with?

    ■ Would you want to work as part of a team or on your own?

    ■ Would you want to travel? If so, how much?

    ■ Would you enjoy a highly structured environment?

    ■ Would you work better in a loosely structured environment?

2. In light of your strengths, weaknesses, gifts, and passions, what kinds of things would you want to be responsible for?

- Do you see yourself in management, sales, marketing?
- Would you enjoy working with numbers, people, or both?
- What kind of assignments would you enjoy tackling?
- Would you enjoy a job that requires a great deal of writing?
- Would you enjoy a job that requires verbal skills?

The reason this exercise is both healthy and helpful is that it allows you to think purely in terms of your passions and abilities. Beginning with a blank page is liberating. It can also be intimidating. We long for structure and boundaries. But boundaries can become walls. Boundaries cause us to sell ourselves short.

Take some time to develop a short job description that you believe would allow you to focus on your core competencies. Those paragraphs will serve as your professional vision—a compass of sorts. The next time you go to a job interview you will have a benchmark by which to measure the appropriateness of the job you are interviewing for.

At the beginning of this section, I stated that as a leader you shouldn't worry about being well-rounded. Instead you should build upon your giftedness and delegate all else. When you do this, the result is a competent organization that reflects your *strengths,* not your *weaknesses.* Helping those around you discover their core competencies and then positioning them accordingly ensures that your organization can perform at peak proficiency.

I mentioned earlier that it is best if I stay away from event planning. That is not something I do well. Yet our organization is known for hosting and producing quality events. Why? Because by stepping out (and staying out!) of that slot, I have created opportunities for people who are gifted in that area to thrive. As a result, people are constantly complimenting me on facets of our organization that I have nothing to do with.

To develop a competent team, help the leaders in your organization discover their leadership competencies and delegate accordingly. There are several ways to do this:

1. Make a list of your key people and write down what you perceive as their primary value to the organization. Having done that, evaluate their job descriptions, asking yourself this question: "How can I free up more of their time to do the things that add the most value to this organization?"

2. Encourage your staff to rewrite their current job descriptions with the goal of refocusing their time on the things they do best.

3. Lead your key people through a discussion of the principles discussed in these three chapters.

4. Create opportunities for your staff to discuss ways to better leverage their abilities.

Having the right people in the right positions is essential to your success and the success of your organization.

There are times when you must pitch in and do things that fall outside your core competencies. But those occasions must be chosen strategically, and they must be the exception, not the rule.

Every December, my father's organization, In Touch Ministries, faces the challenge of shipping thousands of tapes and books to people in time for Christmas. In the days leading up to Christmas my dad shows up at work in blue jeans to help out in shipping. He doesn't show up to run the shipping department. He understands the difference between his responsibilities and his core competencies. He places himself under the authority of those who have expertise in that facet of the organization.

One may wonder: As a leader, is this the best use of his time? Yes and no. For the other fifty-one weeks of the year, the answer is no. If he spent most of his time in shipping, eventually there would be no new product to ship. But for one week of the year it is the absolute best use of his time.

By strategically and temporarily stepping away from the arena where he adds the most value corporately, he steps into an arena where his appreciation is felt personally. Showing up for several hours a day on the assembly line sends a message to every employee about the significance of his or her individual contribution. By becoming "one of the guys" for a week, he enhances his influence with those who follow him once he is back in a coat and tie.

Look for opportunities to temporarily shoulder someone else's burden within your organization. Be strategic in your timing. Remember, once you step outside your zone, don't attempt to lead.

Follow.

Within the context of your current responsibilities and core competencies, what needs to happen to free the majority of your time to do what only you can do? What can you do to expand your 20 percent to 80 percent? In the words of the apostles, what are you currently doing that is "not right"? What's being neglected because your time is now being eaten up with things that fall outside your core competencies?

As you move closer to the ideal, you will become more and more valuable to your organization. As you narrow your focus, you will broaden the opportunities for those who have chosen to follow you. According to Stephen Covey, delegating to others is perhaps the single most powerful high-leveraging activity there is.[8] There are people who love what you hate. Strengthen your team by setting them free to do what only they can do. In that way you will ensure that your organization reflects your strengths as well as the strengths of those around you.

TO BE AN EFFECTIVE LEADER . . .

- Recognize that you have limited strengths. Do whatever it takes to discover what they are. Once you know, find a work environment that allows you to focus your energies on the few things you were created to do well.

- Don't allow your time to get eaten up with responsibilities and projects that call for skills that fall outside your core competencies. That is a recipe for mediocrity.

- Embrace this truth: The less you do, the more you will accomplish.

- Narrow your focus to increase your productivity and expand your influence within your organization.

- Empower the leaders around you by delegating those responsibilities that fall outside your zone. Somebody is dying to pick up the ball you drop. Your weakness is his opportunity.

- Remember: Great leaders know when to follow.

THE NEXT GENERATION CHALLENGE

1. What defines success for you in your current employment situation?

2. Is there alignment between your core competencies and those competencies necessary to succeed in your job?

3. What would change about your current job description if you were given the freedom to focus on the two or three things you do best?

4. What would need to change in your current employment situation in order for you to focus on the things that add the most value to your organization?

5. Take some time to complete the exercises described on pages 36 through 38.

COURAGE
COURAGE ESTABLISHES LEADERSHIP

Chapter Four

FIRST IN

Only those leaders
who act boldly in times of crisis and
change are willingly followed.

[Jim Kouzes]

Leaders love progress. Progress is what keeps them coming back to the task. Nothing is more discouraging to a leader than the prospect of being stranded in an environment where progress is impossible. If we can't move things forward, then it's time to move on.

Progress requires change. If an organization, ministry, business, or relationship is going to make progress, it must change. That is, over time it must evolve into something different. It must become better, more relevant, more disciplined, better aligned, more strategic.

But organizations, like people, resist change. As the authors of *The Leadership Challenge* point out, "Leaders must challenge the process precisely because any system will unconsciously conspire to maintain the status quo and prevent change."[9] Organizations seek an equilibrium. People in organizations seek stability. Both can be deterrents to progress because progress requires change and change is viewed as the antithesis of stability.

Keep in mind that everything you loathe about your

current environment or organization was originally somebody's good idea. At the time it might have even been considered revolutionary. To suggest change is to suggest that your predecessors lacked insight. Or worse, that your current supervisor doesn't get it! Consequently, it is easier to leave things as they are, to accept the status quo and learn to live with it.

While that may be easier, it is not an option for a leader. Accepting the status quo is the equivalent of accepting a death sentence. Where there's no progress, there's no growth. If there's no growth, there's no life. Environments void of change are eventually void of life. So leaders find themselves in the precarious and often career-jeopardizing position of being the one to draw attention to the need for change. Consequently, courage is a nonnegotiable quality for the next generation leader.

Leaders challenge what is for the sake of what could and should be. That's the job of the leader. But challenging what has always been and what has always worked before requires guts. Simply recognizing the need for change does not define leadership. The leader is the one who has the courage to act on what he sees.

Within every church, business, or nonprofit organization in need of change, there is a group of insiders who are keenly aware of the transformations that need to take place. They go home every night and gripe to their spouses. They gather in the break room and complain to each other. But day after day they go about their work resigned to the notion that nothing will change. They are convinced that to try to introduce change would be a costly—and potentially hazardous—waste of time. So they keep their mouths shut and watch the clock. They don't lack insight into what needs to happen; they simply lack the courage to do anything about it.

A leader is someone who has the courage to say publicly what everybody else is whispering privately. It is not his insight that sets the leader apart from the crowd. It is his courage to act on what he sees, to speak up when everyone else is silent. Next generation leaders are those who would rather challenge what needs to change and pay the price than remain silent and die on the inside.

As we will see in the next chapter, simply speaking up has the potential to transform an individual from a mere organizational ornament to an influencer—a leader.

Courage is essential to leadership because the first person to step out in a new direction is viewed as the leader. And being the first to step out requires courage. In this way, *courage establishes leadership*.

We saw this principle at work when we were children. Remember standing around with your friends, daring each other to do something? Then suddenly, somebody went first and everybody followed. The person who goes first is generally viewed as the leader. Courage to act defines the leader, and in turn the leader's initiative gives those around him courage to follow.

There is some question as to whose idea it originally was to put a computer on every desktop. But there is no question about who for years was the leader in the PC industry. The folks at IBM were the first to risk the resources necessary to implement an idea that changed the computer industry forever.

Beyond the need to challenge what should be changed, leaders have been given the assignment to take people places they've never been before.

Leaders provide a mental picture of a preferred future and then ask people to follow them there. Leaders require those around them to abandon the known and embrace the unknown—with no guarantee of success. As leaders we are asking men and women not only to follow us to a place *they* have never been before; we are asking them to follow us to a place *we* have never been before either. That takes guts. That takes nerve. That takes courage.

We all know the fear associated with walking into a dark room or traversing an unlit path. Leading into the future conjures up many of the same feelings. Leadership requires the courage to walk in the dark. The darkness is the uncertainty that always accompanies change. The mystery of whether or not a new enterprise will pan out. The reservation everyone initially feels when a new idea is introduced. The risk of being wrong.

When my children retreat from the darkness of their rooms or the basement, I am quick to remind them that although they are afraid, they are not in danger. As true as that might be, it never helps. Fear defies logic. Information only goes so far. Even when armed with all the reasons why we should not be afraid, the fear remains.

For this reason it is the dark that provides the leader with his greatest opportunities. It is your response to the dark that determines in large part whether or not you will be called on to lead. For the darkness is what keeps the average person from stepping outside the security of what has always been.

Yet many who lack the courage to forge ahead alone yearn for someone to take the first step, to go first, to show the way. It could be argued that the dark provides the optimal context for leadership. After all, if the pathway to the future were well lit, it would be crowded.

Leaders are not always the first to *see* an opportunity. They are simply the first to *seize* an opportunity. It is the person who seizes the opportunity who emerges as the leader. But fear has kept many would-be leaders on the sidelines, while good opportunities paraded by. They didn't lack insight. They lacked courage.

> Leaders are not always the first to see the need for change, but they are the first to act. And once they move away from the pack, they are positioned to lead.

Think for a moment about some of the life experiences you would have missed out on if you had given in to your fear. Chances are you would never have learned to swim or ride a bicycle. You would never have asked anyone out on a date. Most of us men would never have gotten married. We would have cancelled all our job interviews. None of us would be able to ski. Many of us would not have driver's licenses. Unbridled fear results in missed opportunities.

This is a lesson I have rehearsed repeatedly with my children: "If you don't conquer your fear, you are going to miss out on some great things in life."

Often I find myself basically forcing them to try things they would not attempt on their own. Afterwards, we sit down and talk through the dynamic of what took place. In most cases they find that things that began with a lot of fear ended up being a lot of fun.

We have been through this so many times that now they look at me and say, "Is this one of those things we'll be glad we did after it's over?"

Our first white-water rafting trip is a case in point. We were in North Carolina with several other dads and their children. After the outfitter equipped us with life jackets and paddles, he proceeded to go over the dangers of white-water rafting. After about twenty minutes of "What to do in case," my boys were looking at me with that "I'm not so sure about this" look. When he finished, we all packed into the shuttle and headed up the mountain.

The road leading to the spot where we put in ran parallel to the river. Andrew, who was nine at the time, couldn't take his eyes off the rapids. I could tell he was nervous. About fifteen minutes into the trip he turned to me and said, "Dad, I know I'm not going to want to get in the raft when we get there. Just make me do it anyway." I put my arm around him and assured him I would.

"Doing it anyway" is really the only way to ensure that fear doesn't rob you of an opportunity. "Doing it anyway" is the essence of courage. Courage is the willingness to move in a direction in spite of the emotions and thoughts that bid you to do otherwise.

Courage is not the absence of fear. Courage assumes fear. If we had waited for our fear to subside before we took that first plunge off of the high-dive, we would all still be standing there waiting. We just jumped anyway. Courage is the willingness to strap on your fear and move ahead.

The leader who refuses to move until the fear is gone will never move. Consequently, he will never lead. There is always uncertainty associated with the future. Uncertainty presupposes risk. Leadership is about moving boldly into the future in spite of uncertainty and risk. Without courage we will simply accumulate a collection of good ideas and regrets. What could be and should be will not be…at least not under our watch. Eventually somebody else will come along and seize the opportunity we passed up.

Ask veteran leaders about their risk-tolerance and they will all tell you the same thing: "I wish I had taken more risks." In other words, they wish they had not allowed their fear of the unknown to bridle their aspirations. Max De Pree made this observation: "An unwillingness to accept risk has swamped more leaders than anything I can think of."[10]

Seasoned leaders rarely regret having taken risks. Even the risks that didn't pay off directly are viewed as a necessary part of the journey. A leader's regrets generally revolve around missed opportunities, not risks taken. Many of those missed opportunities would not have been missed had they been willing to push through their fear and embrace what could be. Fear, not a lack of good ideas, is usually what keeps a man or woman standing on the sidelines.

Fear of failure is common to man. But leaders view failure differently. Consequently, they don't fear failure in the same way the average individual does.

Here's the difference: *Eventually a leader's lust for progress overwhelms his reluctance to take risks.* In other words, failure to move things forward is the type of failure most feared by the leader. For the leader, failure is defined in terms of missed opportunities rather than failed enterprises.

Failure in any particular enterprise is something a leader can live with. Even laugh about. An unsuccessful enterprise is simply a lesson in things not to repeat. Leaders can much more easily live with the prospects of having tried and failed than not having tried at all. Leaders fear missed opportunity more than they fear an unsuccessful enterprise.

Failure is a part of success. Veteran leaders view failure as simply a necessary chapter in their story: lessons learned, lessons that are essential to future success. Leaders know that failure looks and feels completely different in the rearview mirror than it does when it is staring at us through the windshield.

Ask a successful leader how he overcame his fear of failure, and chances are he won't give you a good answer. Why? Because he has never thought about it. So to the common man, leaders appear to be fearless. The truth is that leaders simply don't fear what other men fear.

Leaders know that the best way to ensure success is to take chances. While the average man or woman fears *stepping out* into a new opportunity, the leader fears *missing out* on a new opportunity. Being overly cautious leads to failure because caution can lead to missed opportunities.

Tom Watson Sr., founder of IBM, understood this principle. A junior executive with the company once managed to lose over $10 million in a venture that was considered risky even by company insiders. When Watson found out about the disaster, he called the young man to his office. Upon entering, the young man blurted out, "I guess you want my resignation?" Watson allegedly responded, "You can't be serious. We've just spent $10 million educating you."[11]

You can't lead without taking risk. You won't take risk without courage. Courage is essential to leadership.

Chapter Five

JUST A STONE'S THROW AWAY

Do not fear, for I am with you;
do not anxiously look about you,
for I am your God. I will strengthen you,
surely I will help you, surely I will uphold
you with My righteous right hand.

[Isaiah 41:10]

Throughout the Old Testament, God instructs kings and military leaders to be courageous and to lead courageously. The Old Testament is full of narratives that illustrate the necessity of courage in the life of the leader. Esther, Joshua, Gideon, Moses…. The list goes on and on. These men and women were given an opportunity to bring about change. And in each case they found that what they needed to leverage their opportunity was *courage*.

Perhaps the youngest Old Testament figure to distinguish himself through an act of courage was David. David was a next generation leader. He was a young man poised to make a difference.

From all outward appearances, though, he was a rich man's forgotten son whose primary duty in life was to tend sheep. But David was a leader-in-waiting. God had gifted him with the skills necessary to lead a nation. Furthermore,

God had chosen him to be the next king. But how do you work your way up from shepherd to king? Besides, everybody knows that the king's son is next in line. Not some filthy shepherd boy.

The thing that makes David's story so relevant to our discussion is the role his courage played in distinguishing him as a leader. David's leadership was established through his courage—not his talent or even his calling by God. David's talent would never have been discovered apart from his courage. One courageous act thrust him onto the stage of national significance in Israel. His courage to act on what he saw was the catalyst that set in motion a long series of providential events.

The event that established David as a leader in the nation of Israel began as a military stalemate between the army of King Saul and the army of the Philistines. The Philistines had gathered their armies for battle about fifteen miles west of Bethlehem on a hill overlooking the Elah Valley. The army of Israel was camped on the other side of the valley. This was pretty typical military strategy: Take the high ground and hope your enemy will take the offensive.

What happened next was a bit unusual, though. The Philistine champion, Goliath, stepped out from among his ranks and challenged Saul to send an Israelite warrior into the valley to meet him for a winner-take-all fight to the death.

He stood and shouted to the ranks of Israel and said to them, "Why do you come out to draw up in battle array? Am I not the Philistine and you servants of Saul? Choose a man for yourselves and let him come down to me. If he is able to fight with me and kill me, then we will become your servants; but if I prevail against him and kill him, then you shall become our servants and serve us." (1 Samuel 17:8–9)

In that day, sending out your best man to do battle with an opposing army's champion was common practice—but for smaller issues like settling border disputes or rights to water. It was unheard of to settle a war between opposing kingdoms in such a fashion. Who in their right mind would risk his entire nation on the combat skills of one warrior? Well, nobody, unless your one warrior was Goliath. Needless to say, nobody in the Israelite army was anxious to become a hero.

Again the Philistine said, "I defy the ranks of Israel this day; give me a man that we may fight together." When Saul and all Israel heard these words of the Philistine, they were dismayed and greatly afraid. (1 Samuel 17:10–11)

While it was true that Goliath represented a significant threat to the security of Israel, he represented something else as well: an opportunity. Wherever there is fear, there is opportunity. Wherever there is great fear, there is great opportunity.

While Saul and his army of combat-hardened veterans were consumed with fear, a young, unknown shepherd saw and seized upon the opportunity.

David's seemingly coincidental arrival at the scene underscores a theme that is repeated in the life of significant leaders throughout history. David did not show up with the intention of becoming a military hero. He was there for an entirely different reason. He was simply delivering grain and bread to his brothers as his father had instructed him to do. He wasn't looking for an opportunity. He was looking for his brothers. But when he saw Goliath, he summoned the courage to exploit an opportunity that other warriors only dreamed about.

As I listen to leaders tell their stories, I hear very little about strategic planning and goal setting. I hear a lot about identifying and acting on opportunities. Strategies and goals have their place. But they don't define leadership. Leaders see and seize opportunity. And in most cases, the opportunities take them by surprise.

So David pushed his way to the front lines of the army just in time to hear Goliath taunt the army of Israel. But he heard something else as well. Saul, in his desperation, had begun offering a reward to any man who would fight and defeat Goliath. By the time David arrived, the ante was pretty high: wealth, the hand of Saul's daughter in marriage, and tax-free living (see 1 Samuel 17:25). All that for killing one soldier who was coming against the armies of God? That was an opportunity David couldn't resist. After double-checking to make sure he'd heard right, David dropped off his package and went to sign up for duty.

What set David apart from every other soldier in Saul's army? It wasn't talent. It wasn't his ability to lead. It wasn't even the fact that he recognized an incredible opportunity. It was his courage to seize what everyone else merely saw. Courage was the catalyst for his leadership.

The next part of the story is somewhat confusing. Why would King Saul send out an untrained shepherd boy to represent his army? It could be that the nature of the challenge required a response, and Saul had no choice but to send the one person who had volunteered.

Whatever the case, Saul was not about to let David go down into the valley looking like a shepherd. So he offered to loan David his armor. When that didn't work out, David assured the king that he would be fine: "The LORD who delivered me from the paw of the lion and the paw of the bear will deliver me from the hand of this Philistine" (1 Samuel 17:37, NIV).

When David left the king's tent, he did something that illustrates a critical distinction often overlooked in discussions related to leadership and courage:

> *He [David] took his stick in his hand and chose for himself five smooth stones from the brook, and put them in the shepherd's bag which he had, even in his pouch, and his sling was in his hand; and he approached the Philistine.* (1 Samuel 17:40)

David was courageous, but he wasn't careless. There is a difference between acting courageously and carelessly. Ask people who work with wild animals, and they will be quick to explain the difference. It takes a great deal of courage to handle a venomous snake. But carelessness could cost you your life.

Leaders worth following are always careful. They are careful because they genuinely care for those who have chosen to follow. A leader who is careless will eventually be considered thoughtless by those who have entrusted their future to him.

David was both courageous and careful. He did not rush down into the valley fueled by adrenaline and the prospects of being a national hero. He wasn't caught up in the moment. He took his time. He took his enemy seriously. And he played to his strengths—namely, a staff and stones.

> Leaders understand the unique roles of confidence and caution. Courage requires both.
>
> David's caution did not keep him from the battle, but neither did he allow his confidence to blind him to the need to select his stones with care.

Unfortunately, fear often disguises itself behind the mask of care. Fearful people often excuse their fear as caution.

"I'm not afraid. I'm just being cautious."

"You can't rush these things, you know."

I doubt very seriously that King Saul or most of his army would have admitted that they were afraid to face Goliath. After all, they were soldiers. But behind their talk of calculated risks and discussions about what was best for the nation, they were just plain scared.

As you evaluate your response to the risks involved in leadership, are you careful or fearful? Every next generation leader must wrestle this question to the ground. What you don't know *can* hurt you. As a leader, what you don't know can paralyze you. Are you consumed by thoughts such as these:

- ■ What if it doesn't work?
- ■ What if I'm wrong?
- ■ What will others think of me?

Take a moment to think through the following five contrasts. Which ones best describe you?

- Careful is cerebral; fearful is emotional.
- Careful is fueled by information; fearful is fueled by imagination.
- Careful calculates risk; fearful avoids risk.
- Careful wants to achieve success; fearful wants to avoid failure.
- Careful is concerned about progress; fearful is concerned about protection.

Saul and his soldiers were fearful. They did nothing. David was careful. He moved forward cautiously. When he was ready, he walked down into the valley alone to face Goliath. And after a brief but intense interchange, David took up his sling and killed the giant.

In that moment two significant things happened. First, there was an instant reversal in the momentum on the battlefield. The army of Israel was suddenly filled with courage and the will to fight. In contrast, the Philistines, who moments before had been beating their chests in defiance, ran for their lives.

When the Philistines saw that their champion was dead, they fled. The men of Israel and Judah arose and shouted and pursued the Philistines as far as the valley, and to the gates of Ekron. (1 Samuel 17:51–52).

David, through his act of bravery, gave an entire army something they severely lacked: courage.

This goes right to the heart of leadership. Leaders instill

courage in the hearts of those who follow. This rarely happens through words alone. It generally requires action. It goes back to what we said earlier: Somebody has to go first. By going first, the leader furnishes confidence to those who follow. In this way, leaders give permission.

In 1991 I made my first pilgrimage to Willow Creek Community Church in Barrington, Illinois. In the months preceding my visit, I had been considering making some major changes in the way I did ministry. But frankly, I was scared. What I was considering was a total departure from the style and philosophy of ministry I had grown up with. Intuitively I knew these changes needed to be made. But I was told by several people I highly respected that this new approach wouldn't work. One fellow assured me that "God won't bless it." Like the army of Israel, I stood on the sidelines longing for the guts to march down into the valley and do what I knew needed to be done.

Those four days in Barrington changed everything. Bill Hybels and his incredible staff did for me what David did for the army of Israel: They gave me the courage to attempt something new. They gave me permission. I just needed to see someone else go first. Once I saw it, I found the courage to follow—and to lead.

As a next generation leader, you will be called upon to go first. That will require courage. But in stepping out you will give the gift of courage to those who are watching. And depending upon the situation, your one act of courage may change the momentum of an entire organization. Courage in a strategic moment can change the playing field dramatically.

Something else of great significance happened in the moment when David toppled Goliath: David became a leader worth following, both in the eyes of those who saw his victory and to those who later heard about his courageous deed. The women of Israel sang of his greatness.[12] The king's son made a covenant with him.[13] And the king started looking over his shoulder.[14] Everybody sensed that there was something special about this boy from Bethlehem. And they were right.

But that something special was present in David before the incident with Goliath. God had called and equipped David to lead. But it took an act of courage for that call to be recognized by the public. Killing Goliath did not make David a leader, but it marked him as one. The incident in the valley of Elah didn't equip David to lead, but it certainly identified him as someone worth following.

What people saw in David had been there all along.

As a next generation leader you already possess the talent and intuition necessary to lead. But chances are it is your *courage* that will establish you as a leader in the minds of others. To put it in perspective, try to identify a leader worth following who didn't pop up on the public radar screen as a result of a decision or action that required courage.

The leaders we revere and imitate walked onto the pages of history through timely displays of courage. Perhaps it was courage on the battlefield or in the boardroom, courage to defend the defenseless, or simply courage to attempt what no one else thought possible. The names and the context change, but throughout the biographies of leaders we consider worth following we find a consistent theme: the courage to act. And in most cases, it was their courage that marked them as leaders in the eyes of the public.

Several years ago I printed out the following question and stationed it in a prominent place in my study so I would be forced to read it every day: *What do I believe is impossible to do in my field…but if it could be done would fundamentally change my business?*

I love that question. It forces me to think outside the realm of what has already been done. What has been done is safe. But to attempt a solution to a problem that plagues an entire industry—in my case, the local church—requires courage. What is currently viewed as impossible—an insurmountable obstacle—is the context for the next paradigm shift in your industry or ministry.

In 1999 the impossible feat facing our church was how to double our worship space in a year without building a worship center twice the size of our current one.

"Huh?"

I'll say it again. We needed to double our worship space in one year in order to keep up with growth. But we did not want to build a worship center large enough to hold twice the number of people. Large worship centers are extremely costly to build and maintain. And when you put two thousand people in a room large enough to accommodate ten thousand, the room feels empty.

So we did something no one else to our knowledge had ever done. We built a second worship center that was identical in size and design to our original one. The two sit back-to-back and are connected at the stages. Through the use of three screens, we have been able to reproduce in our new worship center an exact duplicate of what is happening a few feet away in our original building.

People come from all over the county to see our Siamese

sanctuaries. Why? Because we are the first ones to try this. By being first, we are viewed as the leaders. We aren't the smartest or even the most technologically advanced church around. But we are the first to invest the money and energy in this solution to a problem that many churches face every week.

Our next attempt at tackling the space issue is to build multiple campuses and connect them through technology. We are not the first to attempt this. But the jury is still out about whether this is a viable long-term solution. The only way to know is to try. And instead of waiting around to see if this is a sustainable model, we have chosen to jump in and see if we can make it work.

That's what leaders do. And it requires courage. I'll never forget walking into our second worship center and thinking, *What have we done? We just built two identical auditoriums right next to each other! What if this doesn't work?*

But it did.

Where in your industry, business, or ministry are people perched on the mountainside, staring down into the valley wondering and wishing but not initiating? In your industry, business, or ministry there are opportunities that have not yet been exploited because no one has had the courage to go first.

What are they? Make a list.

As you develop your list, a little voice inside you will whisper, "It will take more than courage to pursue these ideas; it will take capital." At that point you may be tempted to put down your pen and retreat to the safety and comfort of how things have always been done. But before you retreat to your tent, let me remind you of two things: Capital follows courage, and *what* always precedes *how*.

CAPITAL FOLLOWS COURAGE

The courage to dream always precedes the capital needed to finance the dream. Movements, defining moments in industry, breakthroughs in business, all of these begin with courage, not capital. Don't be intimidated by the numbers. If great innovation began with capital, the banking industry would be leading the way in new product development, problem solving, and innovation. That is clearly not the case. Don't be afraid to embrace a problem you cannot afford to solve.

WHAT ALWAYS PRECEDES HOW

The only way to figure out *how* something can get done is to refuse to take your eye off *what* needs to be done. Don't let *how* intimidate you. The fact that *how* is so challenging is the very reason it provides you with great opportunity. As we said earlier, if the pathway into the future were well lit, it would be crowded. If *how* wasn't a problem, somebody else would have already figured it out.

What is impossible to do in your field, but if it could be done would fundamentally change your business?

Somebody needs to be asking that question. Why not you? After all, unsolved problems are gateways to the future. To those who have the courage to ask the question and the tenacity to hang on until they discover or create an answer belongs the future.

Chapter Six

THREE EXPRESSIONS OF COURAGE

Beginning empty-handed and alone
frightens the best of men. It also speaks
volumes of just how confident they are
that God is with them.

[A Tale of Three Kings]

As we pointed out earlier, leadership requires the courage to challenge what is for the sake of what could be. But the need for courage goes beyond the leader's charge to challenge current reality. I want to give you three specific expressions of courage that are essential for those who aspire to be leaders worth following. These three expressions of courage often elude next generation leaders.

1. THE COURAGE TO SAY NO

Early in our development as leaders we assume that when opportunity knocks, we must answer the door and embrace whoever or whatever is standing there. But Mike Nappa was right when he wrote, "Opportunity does not equal obligation."[15] The ability to identify and focus on the few necessary things is a hallmark of great leadership.

In his book *Good to Great,* Jim Collins encourages business leaders to develop a "stop doing" list:

Most of us lead busy but undisciplined lives. We have ever expanding "to do" lists, trying to build momentum by doing, doing, doing—and doing more. And it rarely works. Those who built the good-to-great companies, however, made as much use of "stop doing" lists as the "to do" lists. They displayed a remarkable discipline to unplug all sorts of extraneous junk.... They displayed remarkable courage to channel their resources into only one or a few arenas.[16]

Don't allow the many good opportunities to divert your attention from the one opportunity that has the greatest potential. Learn to say no. The complaint I hear most about young leaders is their inability to focus. A lack of focus eventually translates into a loss of vision. When the vision is fuzzy, people can't follow.

Leaders and organizations that entangle themselves in an array of unrelated "opportunities" dilute their effectiveness. Al Ries, in his groundbreaking book *Focus,* made a similar observation:

It's been my experience that great leaders, in spite of a multitude of distractions, know how to keep things focused. They know how to inspire and motivate their followers to keep pushing "the main chance." They don't let side issues overwhelm them.[17]

Often the reason we won't say no is that we are afraid. We fear disappointing people. We fear being passed by. We fear missing out on a good opportunity. But at some point every leader must come to grips with the fact that there will always be more opportunities than there is time to pursue them. If we don't choose our opportunities carefully, we will dilute our efforts in every endeavor. Refusing to say no eventually robs a leader of his ultimate opportunity—the opportunity to play to his strengths.

Choose your opportunities carefully. Many opportunities are worth missing. Just say no.

2. COURAGE TO FACE CURRENT REALITY

In addition to knowing when to say no, next generation leaders must be willing to face current reality. When someone refuses to face reality, we call it denial. We say that person is sick. The same is true of organizations. Organizations, like individuals, often live in denial. Denial is evidence of an unhealthy organization. Not surprisingly, organizations in denial are usually led by leaders who are in denial about the current state of affairs. They refuse to face the facts. Peter Senge nailed it when he wrote:

> An accurate, insightful view of current reality is as important as a clear vision. Unfortunately, most of us are in the habit of imposing biases on our perceptions of current reality.[18]

As leaders we want to believe that things are good. Our ego and self-esteem are inexorably intertwined with our ability to lead. Life is good when we are leading well. So the tendency, as Senge points out, is to put a positive spin on everything imaginable, while ignoring evidence to the contrary. The danger, of course, is that over time we will lose sight of what is actually happening around us.

The church is a prime example. Every year denominational leaders gather at conventions to compare statistics, hand out awards, and listen to speeches. Over the course of a year, hundreds of millions of dollars are spent on programming and weekly services. All of this is done under the banner of "making disciples" or "transforming lives." But the truth is that there is very little to show for all the meetings, messages, and mothers' mornings out. The church is making far more dinners than disciples. And while there is a general awareness that things are not going well, the average church attendee is content to show up once a week, do his time, and pretend that all is fine.

Author and seminary professor Howard Hendricks was recently asked to assess the declining numbers at a certain church. After attending services he met with the board and made this recommendation: "Put a fence around it and charge admission so that people can come in and see how church was done in the 1950's."[19] In other words, face the facts: You are hopelessly behind.

Leaders worth following are willing to face and embrace current reality regardless of how discouraging or embarrassing it might be. To be that kind of leader, you must be relentless in your quest to know the truth about what is happening around you. You must make it your habit to root out misinformation and refuse to reward those who deliver it. In doing so, you will create a culture that is healthily transparent about what is and isn't taking place.

During World War II, Winston Churchill set up what he called the Statistical Office. The purpose of this organization was to ensure that he received the brutal facts. To protect this unit from the military bureaucracy that surrounded him, he placed the Statistical Office outside his generals' chain of command. He was wise enough to recognize that it would be impossible for him to make good decisions without accurate, and at times painful, information. The same is true for you. But facing the painful truth requires courage.

> Designing and implementing a strategy for change is a waste of time until you have discovered and embraced the current reality. If you don't know where you really are, it is impossible to get to where you need to be. What you don't know can kill you.

It is impossible to generate sustained growth or progress if your plan for the future is not rooted in reality. When time after time your grand strategies don't work out, it is evidence of either low capacity or no interest. In other words, there was something about current reality that you overlooked. Jim Collins says, "Leadership does not begin just with vision. It begins with getting people to confront the brutal facts and to act on the implications."[20] If we are not careful, we will ignore the brutal facts and act instead on what we have convinced ourselves to be true.

Facing current reality is often nasty, but always necessary. Nasty because it may entail acknowledging that you aren't as far along as you thought you were. Necessary because you can't get where you need to be if you don't know where you are to begin with. This is why every successful business or nonprofit turnaround begins with an intense fact-finding mission. Turning an organization around begins with discovering the truth—truth that the previous administration had worked hard to ignore.

To ensure that we are leading with our feet firmly planted on the soil of what *is,* we must live by the seven commandments of current reality:

1. Thou shalt not pretend.
2. Thou shalt not turn a blind eye.
3. Thou shalt not exaggerate.
4. Thou shalt not shoot the bearer of bad news.
5. Thou shalt not hide behind the numbers.
6. Thou shalt not ignore constructive criticism.
7. Thou shalt not isolate thyself.

Attempting to lead while turning a blind eye to reality is like treading water: It can only go on for so long. Eventually you will sink. As a next generation leader, be willing to face the truth regardless of how painful it might be. And if you don't like what you see, change it.

3. COURAGE TO DREAM

Every great accomplishment began as a dream. As one author put it, "All things are created twice. There's a mental or first creation, and a physical or second creation to all things."[21] As a next generation leader, the third expression of courage you must make is to dream about what could be and should be. You must allow your mind to wander outside the boundaries of what *is* and begin to create a mental picture of what *could be.*

The leader who accomplishes great things will not

always be the most talented or the best educated—it will be the leader who refuses to put brackets on his thinking. It will be the leader who refuses to limit himself by what others have done or failed to do.

But dreaming requires courage. For on the heels of every dream is the demon of doubt. No sooner have we latched on to a preferred future than our minds are suddenly filled with all the reasons it won't work. We find ourselves wondering if we are really up to the task. And if we are courageous (or foolish) enough to share the dream with others, they are generally quick to confirm our suspicions.

In spite of all that, we must forge ahead and dream. Otherwise we will simply spend our lives facilitating the dreams of others. If you allow fear to overshadow your dreams, you will never try anything new or create anything new. Worst of all, if fear causes you to retreat from your dreams, you will never give the world anything new.

I keep a little card on my desk that reads, *Dream no small dreams, for they stir not the hearts of men.* More than once, that simple statement has kept me from retreating from my dreams. I know from experience that it is impossible to lead without a dream. When leaders are no longer willing to dream, it is only a short time before followers are unwilling to follow.

So dream! Dream big. Dream often. Somewhere in all those random ideas that flood your mind is one that will capture your heart and imagination. And that seemingly random idea may very well evolve into a vision for your life and leadership.

TO BE AN EFFECTIVE LEADER . . .

■ Leadership is not defined by talent. Look for an opportunity to break with the pack and seize it. Those are the moments in which leadership is discovered and defined.

■ You're afraid. So what? Everybody's afraid. Fear is the common ground of humanity. The question you must wrestle to the ground is, Will I allow my fear to bind me to mediocrity? If so, there is no reason for you to finish this book.

■ Don't let how get in the way of pursuing what. Leaders pursue opportunities long before the means and maps are available. Your industry's unsolved problems are the gateway to the future.

■ Leaders don't hide from the truth. The pain of discovery is the first step on the path to change. If you are going to fear anything, fear not knowing the truth about what's happening around you. In the world of leadership, denial is analogous to receiving the last rites.

■ What could be? What should be? Write it down. Hang it on a wall. Broadcast it.

THE NEXT GENERATION CHALLENGE

1. As a leader what is your greatest fear?

2. How and when does it manifest itself?

3. Do you define failure more in terms of unsuccessful enterprises or missed opportunities?

4. What keeps you standing on the sidelines of opportunity?

5. Do you have a dream that you have put on the back burner for fear of failure?

CLARITY
UNCERTAINTY DEMANDS CLARITY

Chapter Seven

LEADING IN THE SHADOW OF UNCERTAINTY

Every success is usually an admission ticket
to a new set of decisions.

[Henry Kissinger]

Uncertainty is a permanent part of the leadership landscape. It never goes away. Uncertainty is not an indication of poor leadership; it underscores the need for leadership. It is the environment in which good leadership is most easily identified. The nature of leadership demands that there always be an element of uncertainty. Where there is no uncertainty, there is no longer the need for leadership. The greater the uncertainty, the greater the need for leadership. As Jim Kouzes puts it, "Uncertainty creates the necessary condition for leadership."[22]

It took me several years to figure this out. As a young leader I was tormented by the assumption that I should know what to do in every situation. *If I were a good leader,* I would reason, *I would know exactly what to do. After all, I am the leader! Leaders should know. Leaders are supposed to be able to stand up at any given moment and give direction with absolute certainty.* Or so I thought.

Time and experience have taught me differently. So let me say it again: Uncertainty is a permanent part of the leadership landscape. There will be very few occasions when you are absolutely certain about anything. You will consistently be called upon to make decisions with limited information. That being the case, your goal should not be to eliminate uncertainty. Instead, you must develop the art of being clear in the face of uncertainty.

The art of clarity involves giving explicit and precise direction in spite of limited information and unpredictable outcomes. Imagine for a moment that you are the quarterback of a football team. It is fourth and eight. You are six points behind, and five minutes remain on the clock. What do you do? Kick or go for it?

With limited information and facing an unpredictable outcome, you do what every quarterback in that situation does: You draw upon your knowledge and intuition and you call a play. You don't shrug your shoulders and send everybody to the line. You make a decision and send everybody into formation with specific instructions. And when the ball is snapped, you find out whether or not you made the right decision.

As any quarterback will tell you, that kind of clarity requires both confidence and humility. Confidence to move boldly in the direction you have determined. Humility to acknowledge that at best you are making an educated guess.

In the realm of sports we see no conflict between uncertainty and clarity. We are accustomed to coaches, captains, and catchers giving clear signals in the midst of uncertainty. We have seen the chaos that ensues on the playing field when a signal isn't clear. But in the worlds of business, politics, and ministry, uncertainty makes us uneasy. We hesitate. We become less specific and more general in our directives. Our people are unsure of what we expect. We yell "Hike!" and everyone runs in whatever direction he feels is best.

If you're not careful, uncertainty will sand the edges off your clarity. The result will be chaos in the cubicles.

Contrary to what you might think, uncertainty actually *increases* with increased leadership responsibility. The more responsibility you assume as a leader, the more uncertainty you will be expected to manage. The cost of success as a leader is greater uncertainty, not less.

This is why it is imperative for you to learn now how to thrive in uncertain environments. They don't go away. Your capacity as a leader will be determined by how well you learn to deal with uncertainty. Regardless of the type of organization you work in, your future leadership responsibilities will be capped by your ability or inability to manage uncertainty.

As a senior pastor, I deal with more uncertainty than anyone else in our organization. I tell our staff, "I'm responsible for the combined uncertainty of every department in the entire organization." I am responsible for, and at times must deal directly with, the uncertainty in each of our ever-increasing ministry ventures, as well as the sea of uncertainty that surrounds the overall direction of our church. Add to that the uncertainty that goes along with message preparation, and it is a wonder I can think straight. But that's the price of increased leadership responsibility. With success comes greater uncertainty.

To make matters worse, increased responsibility means

dealing with more intangibles and therefore more complex uncertainty. It is the difference between leading a landscaping crew into a yard to do a job on a sunny afternoon and sitting at the helm of a landscaping business that employs twenty-five landscaping crews and trying to determine the best way to market your services. Overseeing the maintenance of a single yard is all about tangibles: shrubs, trees, fertilizer, mowers, arrival, departure. Determining how to market a business is almost completely intangible. It introduces a degree of uncertainty that requires a different kind of leadership.

When we started North Point Community Church, our leadership team was convinced that our adult education program needed to be built around a network of small groups that met in homes. This was in contrast to the adult Sunday school model we had all grown up with. We expected some pushback on this issue. Most of the folks who had committed to helping plant the new church had grown up going to Sunday school. It was all they knew. But we were convinced that a campus-based adult Sunday school program was not the best way to accomplish our mission.

Every time our leadership gathered, the issue of our small-group strategy would come up. Some of our key leaders were not convinced that this was the best route to take. Others assumed we were adopting this strategy only until we had our own facility. People were quick to point out the fact that other churches had tried this approach with limited success.

For a year we listened. We did our best to answer their questions and build consensus among our leaders. We studied what other churches were doing. We piloted about a dozen groups in order to work out the kinks in the system. And then the time came to bring the discussion to a close.

The moment of truth came on a Wednesday evening in a rented facility next door to our property. All of our key adult leadership was present to discuss our plan for moving into our soon-to-be-completed facility. Toward the end of the meeting a woman raised her hand and shared her concern about our small-group strategy. She was genuine, but her question was one I had answered a dozen times before.

In the past I had been diplomatic when this issue came up. This time I put diplomacy aside and was very direct. Understand, these people were my friends. These folks had supported me through the most difficult transition of my life. They were volunteers. These men and women had sacrificed their time and financial resources to ensure a good start. But it was time to call the question. In spite of the uncertainty of our direction, it was time to be clear.

When the woman finished, I smiled and quickly reviewed the discussions we had been having for the previous year. Then I said, "After tonight we are not going to discuss 'if' anymore. We are moving forward. From now on I need you to focus your energies on 'how.' There are many unanswered questions. None of us have ever been part of a church that was organized around home groups. We have a lot to learn. Feel free to question our implementation, but not our direction. As of tonight, we go forward."

That was seven years ago. Currently over five thousand adults are involved in small groups. The men and women who were in attendance that evening became the champions of our small-group ministry. Once it became clear that we were moving forward, everybody got on board.

Were we certain of the outcome? No.

Were we clear about our direction? Absolutely.

> The goal of leadership is not to eradicate uncertainty, but rather to navigate it. Uncertainty is a component of every environment that calls for leadership. Where you find one, you will always find the other.

As you rise through the ranks of leadership, you will be called upon to make decisions regarding ideas, values, purpose, positioning, branding, strategy, and mission. It is all so intangible. Yet eventually these lofty discussions impact reality. In time, the direction you choose for your organization will show up on a bottom line. And there, in the realm of sales, production, recognition, attendance, or whatever your organization is trying to achieve, your leadership will be judged.

One other caveat to keep in mind: In the realm of the intangible, it takes longer to recognize your brilliance or your stupidity. When you make decisions in the realm of business philosophy, values, mission, and marketing, you are forced to lead for long periods of time without the benefit of knowing whether you are actually going in the right direction. By the time the crop starts coming in, it is too late to change your agricultural procedure. You have to wait until the next planting season.

In fall 1998 we moved onto our current church campus. One area of uncertainty for us at that time was traffic flow. We had no history of traffic patterns on our property, yet we had to come up with a plan for efficiently getting cars on and off the campus. As simple as it sounds, it took our team a few days to come up with a plan they felt good about. There was uncertainty. But the good news was that this was all about tangibles: cars, cones, and cops.

On opening day there were some problems. But by the following Sunday, a mere seven days later, the problems were addressed and remedied. Why? Well, partly due to good leadership. But for the most part our parking issues were easy to address because of the context of the uncertainty. We knew immediately what the problems were and how to address them.

We faced a different kind of uncertainty when it came time to determine how to increase our Sunday morning seating capacity. As I said, we eventually decided to build the Siamese sanctuaries, but that was after *two years* of discussion and study.

We found ourselves forced into the world of intangibles: ideas, goals, mission, values, strategy. We discussed our philosophy of ministry and how it impacted people's expectations when they attended our services. We studied attendance patterns and giving patterns.

Yet at the end of the process we had to deliver a mandate to an architect, and eventually there would be a building that hopefully would meet our needs and further our mission. But unlike our traffic decisions, a facility decision is much more permanent (and expensive). The good news is that it seems to have worked out.

Were we certain that our decisions were the right ones? No. If we had waited for absolute certainty, we would still be talking. But a decision had to be made. A clear decision. And that decision, made in the intangible realm of ideas and projections, was eventually judged in the real world of attendance.

Leadership is all about taking people on a journey. The challenge is that most of the time we are asking people to follow us to places we ourselves have never been. There aren't any photographs—we are left with word pictures, metaphors, and illustrations. There are no maps to guide us—we are left to cut a trail. Yet as we move forward into the uncertainty before us, we sense the need to turn occasionally and assure those who follow.

This is the tension every good leader lives with: negotiating uncertain terrain while casting a clear and compelling vision. There is always uncertainty. But uncertainty underscores the need for clarity.

Think for a moment about your leadership environment. How are you managing the uncertainty? As I write these words, I find myself at the helm of the largest church I have ever attended and the only church I have ever pastored. None of my staff has ever ministered in a church this large. In fact, most of my staff have never even worked in a church before.

The truth is that we don't really know what we are doing. This is new for all of us. We have a good idea of where we want the organization to be in five years, but we are absolutely uncertain as to how to get it there. Like you, we have never been to the place we are asking others to follow us to. We will all arrive for the first time together.

But none of that bothers me. I have learned that my enemy is not uncertainty. It is not even my responsibility to remove the uncertainty. It is my responsibility to bring clarity into the midst of the uncertainty. As a next generation leader, that is your responsibility as well.

Chapter Eight

I'LL TELL YOU WHEN WE GET THERE

You can't hold people accountable
for things that aren't clear. If you're unwilling
to make decisions with limited information,
you can't achieve clarity.
[The Five Temptations of a CEO]

Ulysses S. Grant is known for two things: He won the Civil war for Lincoln and he became the eighteenth president of the United States. But he accomplished neither of these achievements because of his great intellect or his superior leadership skills. Ulysses S. Grant is a name we all know because he was the first Northern general who was willing to make difficult decisions and clearly articulate them in an environment of immense uncertainty.

For the first two years of the war, Lincoln was forced to depend upon a passel of opportunistic generals who were more eager for an appointment to leadership than they were the task of leadership. In the early days of the war, Northern generals were so focused on avoiding casualties and embarrassing losses that they would miss strategic opportunities. They spent more time exercising the troops than they did engaging the enemy.

The Union army had superior manpower and equipment, yet they were getting their pants beat off by the genius of Robert E. Lee, a man who did not allow the uncertainty of war to affect his clarity of command.

Ulysses S. Grant was not the most talented or best-educated officer. Prior to the war he had been kicked out of the military for drinking and brawling. His history of reckless personal conduct made it difficult for him to reenlist. But when it became apparent that this conflict was going to last more than a few months, standards on both sides of the aisle were lowered.

Grant was commissioned colonel of the 21st Illinois Volunteers. After his victories at Vicksburg and Chattanooga it became apparent to Lincoln that Grant was the general he had been looking for. Uncertainty did not paralyze him. He was able to give a clear command in the face of unimaginable uncertainty. Within the context of that kind of uncertainty, his clarity of command more than made up for his personal shortcomings. In 1864, Lincoln made Grant commander in chief. In the end he proved to be indispensable to Lincoln.

My point? Ulysses S. Grant was clear even when he was uncertain. He was clear even when he was wrong. The uncertainty of his circumstances did not cloud the clarity of his command. So it must be with you if you are to become a leader worth following.

As leaders we can afford to be uncertain, but we cannot afford to be unclear. People will follow you in spite of a few bad decisions. People will not follow you if you are unclear in your instruction, and you cannot hold them accountable to respond to muddled directives. Neither will they follow if you display a lack of confidence. As you will see later, I am not encouraging you to pretend to be something you are not or know something you don't. But as a leader you must develop the elusive skill of leading confidently and purposefully onto uncertain terrain.

None of us want to be wrong, especially as leaders. But next generation leaders must fear a lack of clarity more than a lack of accuracy. You can be wrong and people will continue to follow. If you are unclear, however, they will eventually go somewhere else. You can survive being wrong. You cannot survive being unclear.

> Our quarters and one-dollar bills serve as a constant reminder that an occasional bad decision will not disqualify you as a leader. People will follow you if you are wrong. They will not follow if you are unclear.

Every great military leader, business leader, and coach has made some bad calls and survived. But even their bad calls were unmistakably clear. There was no doubt in the minds of the soldiers, sales force, or team what it was the general, boss, or coach wanted them to do. The play may have been wrong, but it was executed perfectly because the instructions were clear.

My favorite biblical example of this principle is found in the book of Joshua. Israel was a new nation. Moses was the only leader the people had known. Joshua was his apprentice. The problem was that when the time came for Moses to pass the reins of leadership to Joshua, the leadership environment had changed dramatically. Moses had trained Joshua in the fine art of wandering. For forty years the nation had wandered in the wilderness. Every lesson Moses had taught or modeled for Joshua was related to successful wandering:

- ■ Wandering 101—How to deal with murmurers
- ■ Wandering 102—Proper manna etiquette
- ■ Wandering 103—Snakebite remedies

But the days of wandering had passed. It was time to enter the Promised Land and conquer the people who lived there. As Joshua watched Moses shuffle off to die it must have occurred to him, *I know a lot about wandering, but I don't know much at all about warring.* Talk about uncertainty. No wonder the Lord spoke these words to Joshua: "Have I not commanded you? Be strong and courageous! Do not tremble or be dismayed, for the LORD your God is with you wherever you go" (Joshua 1:9).

There is only one explanation for why God would tell Joshua not to be afraid: He must've been afraid! This was new territory, literally and figuratively. Joshua had never done this before. Everything about the situation reeked with uncertainty. The only thing Joshua knew for certain was that God had said, "Go."

I love the two verses that follow:

Then Joshua commanded the officers of the people, saying, "Pass through the midst of the camp and command the people, saying, 'Prepare provisions for yourselves, for within three days you are to cross this Jordan, to go in to possess the land which the Lord your God is giving you, to possess it.'" (Joshua 1:10–11)

It doesn't get any clearer than that. "In three days we are crossing the Jordan to possess the land." Can you imagine what the people must have thought?

"But Joshua, how are we going to cross the river?"

"I'm not sure, but in three days be ready to go."

"But Joshua, what are we going to do when we get to the other side?"

"I'll tell you when we get there. But in three days we are moving out."

Clear direction in the face of uncertainty. If you are unable or unwilling to be clear when things are not certain, you are not ready to assume further leadership responsibilities.

Before we look at some practical ways to pump up your clarity quotient, I need to warn you about something: The relationship between uncertainty and clarity often creates a potentially dangerous dynamic in the work environment. The individual in your organization who communicates the clearest vision will often be perceived as the leader. Clarity is perceived as leadership.

If you are at the helm of your organization, the application is clear. You must be clear if you are to retain your influence. It is not enough to be the boss. You must be clear. Clarity results in influence.

If you are not *the* leader in your organization, there is another, more complex, application of this axiom: As you gain clarity, you gain influence. At some point your influence may be threatening to those above you who are empowered but not clear. Your clarity may be perceived as disloyalty or an attempt to impose your own agenda. If this dynamic develops, your best move is to take the initiative to assure those in authority that your intention is to further, not compete with, their vision for the organization.

Chapter Nine

MANAGING YOUR UNCERTAINTY

Chaos and uncertainty
are market opportunities for the wise.

[Tom Peters]

Uncertainty is not your enemy. Uncertainty provides you with job security now and unimaginable opportunities in the future. But all of that hinges on your ability and willingness to press on in spite of your surroundings. In this chapter I offer four practical suggestions for enhancing clarity in the midst of uncertainty.

DETERMINE YOUR CERTAINTY QUOTIENT

To begin with, look back at previous decisions and determine the degree of certainty you have achieved in the past.

Think back to your last big decision, preferably one that turned out to be a right decision. How certain were you? At what point did you jump? Were you 100 percent certain? Were you 50 percent certain? At what point were you comfortable pulling the trigger on a decision? Now think back to a time when you chose poorly. How certain were you then? Less than the previous occasion? More?

This is important to know. If in looking back you determine that your best decisions have been made at the

75 percent mark, for instance, then that is your certainty quotient. Generally speaking, you are probably never going to be more than about 80 percent certain. Waiting for greater certainty may cause you to miss an opportunity. Depending upon your personality, no amount of information may move you past a particular degree of certainty.

I rarely get past about 80 percent.

Granted, we are talking about very inexact percentages. There is nothing against which to benchmark your certainty quotient, except maybe the certainty of the leaders around you. But as you think back over your decisions, you will get a general feel for when you operate best.

EXPRESS YOUR UNCERTAINTY WITH CONFIDENCE

In leadership there is always the temptation to pretend to know more than we really do. We fear that people won't follow us unless we portray the image that we are all-knowing.

One reason we fall prey to this way of thinking is that mentally we hang that mantle on the successful leaders around us. We look at them and assume that single-handedly, with no hesitation, they successfully navigate the currents of uncertainty. When we find ourselves in positions of leadership, we feel the pressure to wear that same mantle. "Good leaders always know," we tell ourselves. So when we don't know (which is most of the time) we succumb to the pressure to pretend.

Two things always happen when we pretend. First, we close ourselves off from the input of others. Second, we expose our insecurity to the people we have asked to follow us. The sharp people around you will know when you are bluffing. Pretending erodes respect much quicker than an admission of uncertainty. Uncertainty exposes a lack of knowledge. Pretending exposes a lack of character.

> Saying "I don't know" when you don't know is a sign of good leadership. Pretending to know when you don't know is a sign of insecurity. The only person a pretender deceives is himself.

By expressing your lack of certainty, you give the leaders around you permission to do the same thing. You send them an important message: In this organization it is okay not to know. It is not okay to pretend to know when you don't. As a leader, it is imperative that you know what the people around you know and don't know.

A corporate culture that encourages this kind of honesty and transparency will be a culture that fosters the free exchange of ideas. It will be a learning organization. On the other hand, in an organization where everybody is always expected to know, nobody will ask. When we quit asking, we quit learning.

So how does a leader confidently express his uncertainty? My brother-in-law is a successful real estate broker in the Atlanta area. His mother and father started their company thirty-five years ago. When Rob first got into the business, his mom gave him a jewel of a phrase that he has used ever since. It is the perfect example of confidence in the face of uncertainty: "I don't know, but I will certainly find out."

I will follow a leader who doesn't know but is committed to finding out. So will you. I will not follow a leader who pretends to know and does nothing to quell his ignorance.

Here are some phrases for you to file away for future use:

- "I don't know right now, but I am confident we can figure it out."

- "I don't know right now, but when the time comes to do something about it, I am confident we will have an answer."

- "I don't know, but with folks like you around, I am confident we will come up with a solution."

- "I don't know. I have never done this before. But I think we are up for the challenge."

Don't pretend. You are not a leader because you know everything. Omniscience is not a prerequisite. But confidence is. Express your uncertainty with confidence. When you do, you will instill confidence in those who have chosen to follow.

SEEK COUNSEL

The third thing you can do to make sure you're being clear in the midst of uncertainty is to seek wise counsel. Leadership is not about making decisions on your own. It is about owning the decisions once you make them. If you don't know, ask. If you aren't certain, find out what others are thinking. Consensus builds confidence in the face of uncertainty. When those we respect give us a nod of approval, there is an immediate surge of confidence.

In 1995, after I had concluded that I should plant a new church, I went to see Ron Blue. Ron always knows just the right—and oftentimes uncomfortable—questions to ask. After I went through my spiel about why and where and how, he looked at me, smiled, and said three words that filled me with confidence: "That's good thinking."

I can't tell you what those three words did for me. They didn't erase the uncertainty, but they strengthened my resolve to push ahead.

It is no coincidence that Solomon, the wisest man who ever lived, wrote more about seeking counsel than any other biblical writer. The man who seemed to need it the least was the most convinced of its necessity. The other interesting thing about Solomon's insistence upon seeking counsel is that he was a king. Kings don't need counsel, do they? They are supreme rulers. Throughout the history of Israel, God instated kings who needed counsel. Some sought it. Others did not. Those who did not generally paid a high price in their leadership.

Lesson? Even divinely appointed leaders don't know all they need to know. Again, omniscience is not a requirement for leadership. A willingness to listen is. We will come back to this subject in section four.

MEASURE YOUR SUCCESS BY THE SCOREBOARD, NOT THE PLAYBOOK

Every good coach goes into the game to win. About that he is perfectly clear. And every good coach goes into the game with a strategy, a plan. But every good coach is willing to scrap his plan in order to win. The goal is to win, not to run specific plays. Coaches measure their success by the number of points on the scoreboard, not the number of plays they successfully execute.

Leaders, like coaches, are forced to abandon their plans in order to deliver on the vision. The uncertainty of the landscape will require constant reassessment of your plans. The leader who refuses to scrap or revise his plan rarely reaches his destination.

Clarity of vision will compensate for uncertainty in planning. If you are clear and confident about the destination, you can handle a few detours along the way. If you are unclear about the destination of the journey, even the most sophisticated, well-thought-through strategy is useless.

Chances are that you are more certain about your vision than your plans. The arena of plans and decisions is where leaders face the greatest uncertainty. There will always be an element of uncertainty as it relates to plans. That's to be expected. Plans change; visions remain the same.

Clarity of vision (winning the game) translates into a greater willingness to lead purposefully into uncertain environments. A clear vision, one that has truly gripped our hearts, has the ability to push us through our uncertainty. When I am convinced something must be, I am willing to take chances. In the arena of vision it is always better to try and fail than not to try at all. When a leader is gripped by a clear vision of what could and should be, he will feel compelled to give a clear and certain directive.

As a next generation leader you will be forced to abandon your plans from time to time. Clarify your vision and embrace the uncertainty of your plans. Pencil in your plans. Write your vision in ink.

In the World War II thriller, *U-571,* Matthew McConaughey plays the role of submarine Lieutenant Andy Tyler, who is denied an opportunity to command his own sub. As it turns out, it was his commanding officer, Captain Dahlgren, who encouraged the navy not to promote Tyler.

In a stirring interchange, Tyler challenges his superior officer's decision. He assures the captain that he is qualified. Not only is he able to perform every job on the sub, he goes on to insist that he would be willing to lay down his life for any of the men on the crew.

At that point, Captain Dahlgren, played by Bill Paxton, looks up at the young lieutenant and says, "I'm not questioning your bravery. Are you willing to lay *their* lives on the line?"

Tyler is stunned by the question. Before he can respond, Captain Dahlgren continues:

> You see, you hesitate. As a captain you can't. You have to act. If you don't, you put the entire crew at risk. Now that's the job. It's not a science. You have to be able to make hard decisions based on imperfect information, asking men to carry out orders that may result in their deaths. And if you're wrong, you suffer the consequences. If you are not prepared to make those decisions, without pause, without reflection, then you got no business being a submarine captain.

As Tyler leaves Captain Dahlgren's quarters, the look on his face says it all. Peering at leadership through that particular lens has caused him to doubt his readiness to lead.

Uncertainty will not be your undoing as a leader. However, your inability to give a clear directive in the midst of uncertainty might very well be the thing that takes you out or causes you to plateau early in your career.

TO BE AN EFFECTIVE LEADER . . .

- Be clear even when you are not certain. The only thing we can be certain about is the past—everything from this moment on is a guess. Once you acknowledge that, you will be free to make decisions with limited information.

- Recognize that clarity of vision is more important than certainty of outcome. Every great accomplishment began as an idea that stood in contrast to someone's current reality. In the beginning there is always enough uncertainty to shut down a vision—thus the need for leadership.

- Remember that clarity is perceived as leadership. Clarity creates its own influence and its own momentum. Whoever paints the clearest picture will ultimately be viewed as the leader.

- Don't pretend. Once you are okay with what you don't know, the people around you will be okay with it as well. One of the worse things you can do as a leader is to pretend that you have all the answers; to do so is to unnecessarily jeopardize your mission.

- Be flexible. Uncertainty will wreak havoc with your plans, but don't allow uncertainty to derail your vision. Pencil in your plans. Etch the vision in stone.

THE NEXT GENERATION CHALLENGE

1. Are you clear in your directives?
2. Has the uncertainty of your environment taken the edge off of your clarity?
3. What is more harmful to those in your organization: clear directives that are changed midstream or unclear directives that are difficult to follow?
4. Can everyone in your organization answer these questions:
   - What are we doing?   • How do I fit in?
5. How easy is it for you to own your bad decisions?

COACHING

COACHING ENABLES A LEADER
TO GO FARTHER, FASTER

Chapter Ten

LISTENING, LEARNING

I believe providing feedback is the
most cost-effective strategy for improving
performance and instilling satisfaction.

[Ken Blanchard]

In 1972 the youth director in our church decided to reward our church basketball team with a trip to Disney World. I'm not sure why any rational adult would want to take eight teenage boys anywhere for an overnight trip. But then again, Mary Gellerstedt was known for taking chances.

Anyway, I have three distinct memories from that trip: playing war in the orange grove next door to our hotel, hearing "Tiny Dancer" by Elton John for the first time and deciding it would be my favorite song for life, and teaching Scott Ward how to do a one-and-a-half flip with a twist at the hotel pool.

Scott Ward was and still is the most fearless individual I know. After returning from an exhilarating day at the park, we all headed for the pool. While the rest of us were content simply to get in the water, Scott decided he would use the time to master the one-and-a-half with a twist.

His first attempt was dismal. A cry arose from the seven of us when Scott did a face plant. As he was making his way back to the diving board, I suggested that he tuck a little tighter and release a little sooner. He did. And as a result, he almost escaped his second attempt without any pain.

This went on for an hour: Scott sacrificing his body and me making suggestions. Before long, Scott had just about mastered a one-and-a-half with a twist. It wasn't pretty. But it wasn't painful either.

As he approached the board for the last time, our youth director said, "Andy, I didn't know you were a diver." I assured her that I wasn't. Scott stopped halfway up the ladder and gave me a rather perplexed look. "You mean you can't do this yourself?" I just shook my head and laughed. "Are you kidding? I wouldn't even try." At that point, Scott decided to forgo his last attempt, pick me up, and throw me in the pool.

That was my first experience as a coach. And from that experience I learned a valuable lesson: Never suggest anything to Scott Ward that you are not willing to try yourself.

Actually, I took two things away from that experience:

1. I can go farther and faster with someone coaching me than I can on my own.

2. An effective coach does not need to possess more skills than the person he is coaching.

You will never maximize your potential in any area without coaching. It is impossible. You may be good. You may even be better than everyone else. But without outside input you will never be as good as you could be. We all do better when somebody is watching and evaluating.

I read an interview recently with Gil Reyes, Andre Agassi's conditioning coach. The notion of Agassi having a coach seems a little strange in itself. Why would he *need* a coach? What more could he possibly learn about the game of tennis? And what could he learn from a guy who is not as good as he is on the court? The answer: plenty. Andre knows what every great athlete knows. To be the best he can be, he needs input from someone else.

In the interview, Agassi didn't hold back from paying tribute to Reyes:

> For me it's immeasurable how much Gil has impacted my career, especially as I get older. Like any profession, [tennis] requires some subtle judgments that are crucial. Gil, in my opinion, is the first in the world at making those decisions.[23]

At the end of the article, the writer makes this observation: "As the months and years go by and age becomes more of an obstacle in Agassi's life, Reyes's influence will be even more valuable."

Agassi is wise enough to recognize that age and experience do not diminish his need for a coach. In fact, the opposite is true. Age and experience don't necessarily make us better. Age and experience have a tendency to leave us in a rut, doing the same thing the same way with no one around to spur us toward change.

Think about it: Every top athlete and athletic team has a coach. In the world of athletics, nobody performs his way out of needing a coach. In the world of leadership, however, we operate under the misguided assumption that because we are leaders, we don't need to be led. Once we are recognized for our ability to "perform," we think we don't need outside input in order to enhance our performance. Consequently, we measure our leadership against what others are doing rather than against our God-given potential. And in the end we never become all we could have been.

> To be the best next generation leader you can be, you must enlist the help of others. Self-evaluation is helpful, but evaluation from someone else is essential. You need a leadership coach.

We have a tendency to measure ourselves against the people around us. They become our point of reference. A good coach will evaluate your performance against your potential. A coach helps you measure your performance against your strengths instead of against someone else's. A coach will know what you are capable of and will push you to your limit.

During my junior year of college I took an advanced speech class with the chairman of the department, Dr. Rifkin. He was a great teacher and highly respected among the faculty and students. While I don't remember too much from his lectures, I'll never forget what he said when I challenged him on the grade he gave me on my first speech.

There were about fifteen people in the class. Each of us was to give a persuasive speech on a topic of our choice. Public speaking came easy for me. But that was clearly not the case with most of the students in the class. In fact, some of their presentations were dreadful at best. I don't remember my topic, but I do remember thinking how much better my speech was than most everybody else's in the class.

A couple of days later Dr. Rifkin returned our outlines

with our grades. I just happened to notice that the fellow to my right had made a B+ and the girl sitting behind me had made an A-. Compared to their presentations I deserved an A.

When Dr. Rifkin handed me my outline, I was shocked to see that I had received a B. A *B?* That was impossible. There was no comparison.

After class I marched up to the front of the lecture hall to plead my case. Dr. Rifkin listened patiently, smiled, and said, "You are capable of far more than you gave us today."

He was right. I was winging it. Like a good coach, he wasn't grading me on the basis of how everyone else had performed. He was grading me on the basis of what he perceived as my potential.

Defining the role of a coach in the field of athletics is made easy due to the fact that most of us have been coached athletically somewhere in our past. Beyond that, many of us have found ourselves with a whistle around our own necks. For some, a chance to coach their child's baseball or soccer team is viewed as a great opportunity. In my case it was the result of Sandra's assumption that by signing me up as a soccer coach I would have more quality time with our boys. The fact that I didn't know the first thing about soccer was beside the point. She saw it as a great opportunity. And in the end I agreed.

Defining the role of a coach in the realm of leadership is more challenging. For one thing, leadership coaches are not as visible. Unlike some basketball coaches who are often seen running up and down the court barking out instructions to their players, the leadership coach operates behind the scenes. Unlike the real-time, in-game coaching in the world of athletics, the leadership coach makes his presence known only before and after the game.

Consequently, there are men and women in the marketplace and in ministry whom we look up to with the false assumption that they "made it" on their own, that they are what they are because of talent and discipline alone. As you probe deeper into their stories, however, you will find that each one often had one or two key people who coached them to success.

One of the best ways to understand the role of a leadership coach is to compare coaching to three familiar disciplines: counseling, consulting, and mentoring.[24]

COUNSELING

The job of a counselor is to help an individual resolve issues of the *past* in order to operate more effectively in the *present*. A coach, on the other hand, helps us assess the *present* so that we can operate more effectively in the *future*.

CONSULTING

A consultant is typically engaged for a short time in order to solve a specific problem. A coaching relationship is typically a medium- to long-term prospect. Coaching does not center on problem solving, as it is with consulting. Instead the focus is performance enhancement.

MENTORING

A mentor is usually an older and more experienced person who provides advice and support to a younger, less experienced individual in a particular field. Coaching encompasses all the components of a mentoring relationship, and then some. The primary difference is that in a coaching relationship, the coach often takes more initiative about when and how information is passed along.

Unlike a typical mentoring arrangement, a leadership coach doesn't simply advise when asked. A coach is going to be more proactive in his instruction and evaluation. A coach is often on the scene watching rather than in an office waiting for a report.

In the world of athletics, the coach does not withhold his opinion until asked. Neither does he sit back and watch his protégé make the same mistake over and over without saying something. In the same way, a good leadership coach will do everything in his power to ensure progress. Like an athletic coach, a leadership coach operates as if he has something on the line. A win for the man or woman he is coaching is a win for himself as well. Wins and losses are personal. Good leadership coaches function as if they have something at stake in your performance.

As obvious as that sounds, there is something in many of us that resists being coached in the realm of leadership. We are willing to spend outrageous amounts of time and money perfecting our putts, serves, and swings. But when it comes to our leadership, we resist input. Maybe it's the way leaders are wired. Maybe it's pride. I don't know. But on more than one occasion I have interfaced with young leaders who had great potential but who were unteachable.

In the next chapter we will take a look at what can happen when a leader refuses to submit himself to the counsel of others.

Chapter Eleven

THE KING WHO WOULDN'T LISTEN

Let the wise listen and add to their learning,
and let the discerning get guidance.

[Proverbs 1:5, NIV]

Great leaders are great learners. But learning assumes an attitude of submission. And submission isn't something all leaders are comfortable with. Submission is what others, those people who need to be led, do. Our strengths can easily become our weaknesses. And so it is with a leader's attitude toward submission. This is especially true in the early years of a next generation leader's life—those years when we are sure we already know everything and all we need is an opportunity to prove it.

Engaging a leadership coach requires a willingness on the part of a leader to submit to the counsel and instruction of others. *If you are not teachable, you are not coachable.* Unfortunately, the younger we are, the more we think we know and the less likely we are to genuinely place ourselves under the influence of a leadership coach. This is especially true if we view ourselves as more capable, passionate, or talented than the people around us.

This is why I have always been fascinated by the fact that Solomon, the wisest man who ever lived, wrote so much about seeking wise counsel. As we noted in the previous section, he had more to say about the importance of wise counsel than all the other biblical writers combined.

Think about it: Why would the man who needed it least recommend it most?

Simple: He was the wisest man in the world. *Wisdom seeks counsel.* The wise man knows his limitations. It is the fool who believes he has none. Only the naïve would operate under the assumption that he can make all the right calls without input from the outside.

Here are a few of Solomon's thoughts on seeking counsel:

- Let the wise listen and add to their learning, and let the discerning get guidance. (Proverbs 1:5, NIV)

- The way of a fool seems right to him, but a wise man listens to advice. (Proverbs 12:15, NIV)

- Plans fail for lack of counsel, but with many advisers they succeed. (Proverbs 15:22, NIV)

- Listen to advice and accept instruction, and in the end you will be wise. (Proverbs 19:20, NIV)

The value of surrounding oneself with wise counselors was something Solomon was able to pass along to his son, Rehoboam. The value of *listening* to their wise counsel, however, was not. Rehoboam's unwillingness to heed the advice of those who were older and wiser cost him dearly.

Following the death of King Solomon, the people of Israel gathered together in the city of Shechem to crown his son, Rehoboam, king. Before the coronation, however, the people appointed Jeroboam to make a simple request of the young heir to the throne: "Your father made our yoke hard; now therefore lighten the hard service of your father and his heavy yoke which he put on us, and we will serve you" (1 Kings 12:4).

In the latter years of Solomon's reign, Rehoboam had strayed from the path of wisdom. In those days, Solomon became obsessed with making Israel an epicenter of culture. He accomplished this primarily through an aggressive building campaign. The citizens of Israel bore the brunt of his ambition. Their taxes were high and they were forced to allocate an unrealistic amount of time to the construction. Even as loyal subjects to the king and citizens of Israel, they were reduced to the status of slaves.

After Solomon died, the people wanted a break. So they came to Rehoboam to pledge their support, provided he would lead differently than his father.

Rehoboam responded wisely:

> *Then he said to them, "Depart for three days, then return to me." So the people departed. King Rehoboam consulted with the elders who had served his father Solomon while he was still alive, saying, "How do you counsel me to answer this people?"* (1 Kings 12:5–6)

So far so good. Rehoboam gave himself some time and he invited other people into the decision-making process. His daddy had taught him well.

And notice who his coaches were: "the elders who had served his father." Again, good decision. His father's advisers were perfectly positioned to coach him through this decision-making process. They had the advantage of age as well as the opportunity to observe and give input.

Here's what they said:

Then they spoke to him, saying, "If you will be a servant to this people today, and will serve them and grant them their petition, and speak good words to them, then they will be your servants forever." (1 Kings 12:7)

Rehoboam's advisers knew that great leaders are great servants. This was something Solomon had lost sight of in his twilight years. Now Rehoboam had the opportunity to recapture the hearts of the people. In sharp contrast to his father, he could actually lead the people rather than simply rule them.

But, like many of us when we are young and oh so smart, Rehoboam was unwilling to listen. He was not interested in serving anyone. Such advice must have sounded like the babbling of old men whose day had come and gone. Besides, what had they ever led? Whom had they ever ruled?

Next generation leaders must realize that it is not the *accomplishments* of a coach that make him a valuable ally in the endeavor of leadership. Most of the time it is not even what a coach *knows* that makes him valuable. It is what he *sees* that counts.

The elders could see something Rehoboam could not see. They saw a group of men and women eager to follow. They saw a young king who did not understand the relationship between privilege and responsibility.

The wise leader listens to wise counsel. Where does the next generation leader find wise counsel? From those who have the advantage of age and the opportunity to observe.

Herein is the power of coaching. Had Rehoboam listened, he would have gone farther as a king faster. He would have led his kingdom beyond his natural ability and maturity. By listening to those who had the advantage of age and observation, he would have established himself as a wise and trustworthy leader in the minds of the people.

But that's not what happened:

> *But he forsook the counsel of the elders which they had given him, and consulted with the young men who grew up with him and served him.*
>
> *So he said to them, "What counsel do you give that we may answer this people who have spoken to me, saying, 'Lighten the yoke which your father put on us'?"*
>
> *The young men who grew up with him spoke to him, saying, "Thus you shall say to this people who spoke to you, saying, 'Your father made our yoke heavy, now you make it lighter for us!' But you shall speak to them, 'My little finger is thicker than my father's loins! Whereas my father loaded you with a heavy yoke, I will add to your yoke; my father disciplined you with whips, but I will discipline you with scorpions.'"* (1 Kings 12:8–11)

Rehoboam's friends had no more wisdom or perspective than he did. Rehoboam was blinded by power, and they were equally blinded by the prospects of being close to the man in power. They told him what he wanted to hear, and he went with it.

Three days later the people reconvened. Rehoboam gave them his answer. He said he would lead in such a way as to

make them long for the days of his father. He was not there
to serve; he was there to rule!

In making such a bold claim, Rehoboam was assuming
something that many a leader has wrongly assumed. He
assumed that his position alone would ensure the loyalty of
the people. He wasn't mature enough to understand that
every follower is a volunteer. Abuse your position as leader
and you will lose those you lead. Nobody *has* to follow. You
can't force people, even subjects, to follow. You might be
able to force them into submission, but you can't force them
to become loyal followers.

> We can rent their hands, arms, legs, and backs, and
> the market will help us to determine the rent we will
> pay. But are they not volunteers in even the strictest
> sense of the word? Are they free to leave? Can they
> go across the street to another employer for an extra
> fifty cents an hour? Or even fifty cents less if they
> really don't like us? Of course they can. And what
> about their hearts, minds, commitment, creativity,
> and ideas? Are these not gifts that must be volun-
> teered? Can you order or demand commitment?
> Excellence? Creativity?[25]

Generally speaking, people don't follow rulers. They
follow *leaders*. Rehoboam learned this the hard way.

> *When all Israel saw that the king did not listen to
> them, the people answered the king, saying, "What
> portion do we have in David? We have no inheritance
> in the son of Jesse; to your tents, O Israel! Now look*

after your own house, David!" So Israel departed to their tents. (1 Kings 12:16)

Upon hearing Rehoboam's leadership strategy, ten of the twelve tribes of Israel decided not to follow. He heeded the advice of those who told him what he wanted to hear, and the result was a revolution. And there wasn't one thing Rehoboam could do about it. In his rush to rule he lost the opportunity to lead. He lost the very thing he was attempting to preserve. What should have been his moment of greatness devolved into his most embarrassing moment. By posturing himself as a mighty king, he lost his kingdom. He had the opportunity to be the next king of Israel and he let it slip through his fingers.

All because he was unwilling to listen to the counsel of those who were there to help him go farther, faster.

When we were developing plans for our first worship center, I told our architect not to include a baptistery. In my experience baptism was always tacked on to the beginning or the end of a service. There was never an opportunity for the people being baptized to tell their stories. It always seemed rushed. And other than the family of those being baptized, nobody else really seemed that interested in what was going on.

I wanted our baptism services to be a time of celebration. So I thought the best thing to do would be to build an outdoor baptismal pool. Our executive staff—all of them about my age—thought this was a great idea. The six of us were convinced that by putting the baptistery outside we would breathe fresh life into this sacred ordinance.

When I presented the building plans to our elders—all of whom were older than I—one of the first questions they asked was, "Where's the baptistery?" I smiled and launched into my well-rehearsed explanation of why it would be a mistake to put the baptismal pool in the worship center. I sensed that this was going to be a hard sell, so I did my best to paint a picture of how exciting it would be to gather around an outdoor pool and celebrate as people were coming up out of the water.

The eleven men in attendance that night listened patiently to my impassioned plea. Then one by one they voiced their opposition to my "brilliant" idea. After several minutes of discussion we voted. The final vote was eleven to one in favor of including the baptistery in the worship center.

I left the meeting convinced that we had just voted to build something we would never use. I was confident that once we got into our building they would see the light and agree to an alternate site for baptism. While I had great respect for these men, I had a hunch that their appreciation for tradition had clouded their thinking. In the end, I told myself, they would come around to my way of thinking.

One week later our architect brought me the new plans for the worship center, complete with indoor baptismal pool. His drawings confirmed my fear. The contemporary design of our worship center did not lend itself to a centrally fixed baptistery. Consequently, he was forced to situate it over to one side. It threw the whole room out of balance. I was really frustrated. Not only were we spending money to build a baptistery that we would never use, it was going to mess up the whole look of the building.

I was really tempted to do an end run around the elders'

decision. But I had been brought up believing that God works through channels of authority. And like it or not, the elders, not me, were the authority over the church. So I threw up my hands and just let it go. After all, we could always use it for a puppet stage.

Now, five years later, when I think back on how close I came to ignoring the advice of that discerning group of men, it makes me feel sick. Baptism is the highlight of our morning worship service. People clap, cheer, whistle, stand, hug, cry. It really is unbelievable.

Everyone who is baptized at North Point is required to give a two- to three-minute videotaped testimony of why he or she is being baptized. These are shown immediately preceding each baptism. There are many Sundays I just want to close the service after baptism. The stories say it all. And every time someone steps into those waters, I am reminded of how wrong I was and how foolish it would have been for me to manipulate the system in order to have my way.

I have more in common with Rehoboam than I would like to admit. Chances are, you do too. When I make up my mind about something, I don't really want anyone telling me it is not a good idea. Every leader I know leans in that direction. So God, in His wisdom, has placed men and women around us with the experience and discernment we often lack.

If we are wise enough to listen, they will help us go farther, faster.

Chapter Twelve

WHAT COACHES DO

Coaches focus on future possibilities,
not past mistakes.

[John Whitmore]

So what exactly does a leadership coach do? Three things. An effective leadership coach:

1. Observes

2. Instructs

3. Inspires

It is just about impossible to help someone become a better performer if you never actually see him perform. It would be difficult to coach a pitcher if you never saw him pitch. It would not be feasible to coach a gymnast if you never watched her do her routine.

The same is true in leadership. The person or people you invite into the role of coach must be in a position to watch you lead.

The thought of having someone evaluate your leadership may be intimidating at first. But think about it: People watch you lead all the time. Leadership doesn't happen in a closet. It is a public performance. Our leadership is constantly on display. As leaders we are on a stage in front of all those who have chosen to follow us. So why not plant a coach or two among the crowd?

My first "observer" was Nolen Rollins. I didn't know it at the time, but Nolen was one of the best leadership coaches I ever had. Nolen was my supervisor during my tenure as a student minister. Most bosses don't coach. They reward and reprimand. (Unfortunately, most parents fall into the same routine as well.) But Nolen was different. He assumed the role of coach. When I say he "assumed" that role, I mean he didn't wait for me to ask—he just jumped in. He was not content to merely reward and reprimand. He took it upon himself to develop me as a leader.

Nolen took the time to observe me in just about every leadership role I assumed. He sat in on my leadership meetings, he attended my staff meetings, he would even slip into our student programs and listen to me communicate. From time to time he would ask me to lead our general staff meetings. And he would just sit back and observe.

Once a week or so, Nolen would drop by my office, sit down, and tell me what he had observed. He was kind, but direct. He didn't pull any punches. The fact that Nolen spent so much time observing me made it easy for me to listen and embrace his comments. I knew he was on my side. He wasn't simply critiquing; he was coaching. He was helping me go farther, faster.

In addition to observation and evaluation, you need instruction. Good leadership coaches are teachers.

For several years I met once a week with a fellow named Charlie Renfroe. Charlie is a successful businessman and a wonderful father and husband. Charlie coached me in the arena of professional and personal relationships. He taught me how to negotiate a deal, confront people who were underperforming, and reward those who were going the extra mile.

The unique thing about Charlie was that he instructed me primarily through stories drawn from his own journey. I would ask a question and Charlie would tell a story. Then he would look me in the eye and tell me exactly what he would do if he were in my shoes. Space does not permit me to share all the rich insights I gained from Charlie during our Tuesday mornings together, but his stories helped me become a better leader. Even now when I might be on the verge of reverting to some unhealthy leadership pattern, I'll remember one of Charlie's stories, and it will stop me in my tracks.

One particular morning I was describing to Charlie a situation that involved my supervisor. I had inadvertently made a decision that contradicted a decision he made the previous day. Word had gotten back to me that he was pretty ticked. And understandably so. As a result of my action it looked like there was division in his department. I mentioned to Charlie that I wasn't looking forward to going to the office. Then I made the mistake of saying that I was actually thinking about not going in at all.

Charlie immediately launched into a story about a situation he had been in with some bankers in New York. He had leveraged his company beyond what was reasonable or wise. Then for no apparent reason, revenues started falling. Before long he was upside down with the bank. Normally when that happens, the lenders start calling and the lendees are hard to find. Charlie took the opposite tack. He called and made an appointment with the bank and flew to New York to meet with them.

As he tells it, "I let 'em know that they could count on me to work this thing out and that they were never going to have to come looking for me because I was going to flood them with progress reports. They weren't sure what to do with that. I called 'em every week to let them know how things were going. They have been after me for more business ever since."

Then he said something I'll never forget: "The best thing to do sometimes is to open up the cage and face the five-hundred-pound gorilla. He's going to come after you anyway, so you might as well let him out." Then Charlie leaned in, looked me square in the eye, and said, "When you get to the office, you go directly to your supervisor's office. Open the cage and face the five-hundred-pound gorilla."

That's exactly what I did. And I've been opening cages ever since.

> A good leadership coach will do everything in his power to help you close the gap between your potential and your performance. That may entail brutal honesty. Why? Because the painful truth is the fast track to increased performance.

The third component of a good leadership coach is inspiration. A good coach will be able to instill in you a mental image of what could and should be true of you as a leader. He will point you toward a preferred future and inspire you to do everything in your power to achieve it.

A good coach always coaches to a leader's potential, not

his current level of performance. A good leadership coach will see the potential in you and inspire accordingly.

Currently I am being coached by a retired pastor. John is a member of our church, a fact that gives him an opportunity to observe me in a communication and visioncasting role. One day he looked at me across the lunch table with concern and said, "Andy, your endings are weak."

I knew exactly what he was talking about. For several Sundays our worship services had been landing hard. We had been putting a lot of planning into how we started our services but very little thought or creativity into our closings. He was exactly right.

But John didn't stop there. He knew I had the potential to do better, so he spent several minutes casting a vision for what could and should be. He referred back to specific instances when we had closed with as much intensity and intentionality as we had opened with. I walked away committed and inspired to do better.

The following Monday in our service-planning meeting I announced, "Our endings have been weak." Everyone agreed, and we went to work remedying the problem. Two weeks later Sandra and I bumped into John after church at a restaurant. He was sitting at a table with several other people. Through the cross-talk around the table, John caught my eye and gave me a thumbs up, slowly nodding his head, signifying that we got it right.

John makes me feel like I could conquer the world. Never in my life have I had anyone address so consistently and persuasively what I could and should be. I always walk away from those coaching sessions more passionate about reaching my potential as a leader, father, and husband. That's what good leadership coaches do.

Now let's talk about how you can find a leadership coach for yourself.

Engaging a good leadership coach is difficult, for two reasons. To begin with, most people won't even know what you are talking about if you ask them to serve as your leadership coach. Second, qualified candidates will tell you they aren't qualified.

So here's what you've got to do: Don't ask anyone to coach you. That will scare them off. The word *coach* implies preparation and training. More than likely the men or women you target as potential coaches don't have time to prepare anything or develop a training program.

So stay away from that term and instead ask them to evaluate a specific facet of your leadership. Most people love to evaluate. Basically you are asking them for their opinion. Who doesn't love to give his opinion? If you have chosen wisely, the opinion and input of that individual will turn out to be quite valuable.

The important thing at this point is to be specific. For example, you could ask someone on your leadership team or board to evaluate the way you conduct meetings. Say something like the following:

"We have both had to sit through our share of poorly run meetings, all the time thinking, 'Why doesn't he just get to the point?' or 'Why won't she let somebody else talk?' We both know that leaders often have no idea how they are coming across in meetings or decision-making environments. This is one area in which I really want to improve. I would love to get together sometime and get your take on how I am doing as the moderator of our meetings. I'm open to any suggestion you make. If you are aware of unhealthy dynamics in the group, I would love to get your input on that as well."

You have not asked for any long-term coaching relationship. You have simply asked for input. If your evaluation time with this person proves beneficial and enjoyable, chances are you have found a coach.

Once we invite someone into the role of evaluator he generally feels the freedom to remain in that position until we tell him otherwise. In other words, if someone agrees to an invitation similar to the one outlined above and he feels like you took his input seriously, you shouldn't be surprised if he initiates the next meeting. Once that happens, you've got yourself a coach. He's not only observing, but also instructing.

Now, before you write off this exercise as something reserved for the novice leader, let me assure you that this kind of assessment is appropriate throughout our term as leaders. The reason seasoned veterans don't seek out leadership coaches has nothing to do with their actual need of a coach. It has everything to do with their perceived need.

Remember, you are being evaluated all the time. This is just one way of discovering what everybody is thinking (and whispering) anyway. Experience alone doesn't make you better at anything. By itself, experience has the potential to leave you in a rut. Evaluated experience is what enables you to improve your performance.

The following is a list of leadership environments in which you might consider inviting a leadership coach to observe and evaluate your performance:

- meetings
- public presentations
- decision-making
- visioncasting
- writing
- conflict resolution
- personnel selection
- strategic planning
- budget development

Learn everything you can from everybody you can. Learn everything you can about yourself from anybody who will pause long enough to observe and evaluate. Look for an environment where you will be coached, not just paid. In the early years of your career *what you learn is far more important than what you earn*. In most cases, what you learn early on will determine what you earn later on.

As a leader, what you don't know can hurt you. What you don't know about yourself can put a lid on your leadership. You owe it to yourself and to those who have chosen to follow you to open the doors to evaluation. Engage a coach.

While you are looking for a leadership coach, go ahead and become a coach for another leader around you. I know, I know: You are too young; you wouldn't know what to say; nobody is going to take you seriously; blah, blah, blah.

Forget all of that. Even if you have to begin with your assistant or even a peer, you can coach. Begin by passing along pertinent articles, books, tapes. Comment in detail about the things they are doing right. Brag about 'em. Talk about their potential. And once you have won their trust, evaluate and inform. Use the phrase, "One thing I learned a long time ago is…." In other words, position yourself as a fellow learner, not a teacher.

Don't wait until you feel adequate. Leaders are learners. Consequently, leaders rarely feel adequate to teach others to lead. As learners, they are constantly reminded of all they have yet to learn and master.

Don't miss this: As a leader, you are not responsible for knowing everything there is to know about leadership. But you are responsible for sharing what you do know with the leaders around you. And as you pour into their cup what God and others have poured into yours, they will go farther, faster too. They will be better leaders for having known you.

Get a coach and you will never stop improving.

Become a coach and ensure the improvement of those around you.

TO BE AN EFFECTIVE LEADER . . .

■ Face it, you are not as good as you could be. So what are you going to do about it? The only way to go farther, faster, is to engage outside help. You can maximize your leadership potential by getting a coach...or two.

■ Find someone to observe you in a variety of leadership settings. Outside input is critical. Even if you could watch yourself in a mirror twenty-four hours a day, you would never see yourself as others see you.

■ Select a coach who has no axe to grind and no reason to be anything except brutally honest. He need not be an expert in your field. What your coach must be able to do, however, is put himself in the shoes of those who are influenced by your leadership.

■ Try to find someone who can articulate his thoughts with clarity and precision. You don't need glaring generalities; you need to know exactly what needs to be repeated and deleted in your leadership.

■ Become a coach. As we learn to do by doing, we learn to accept by giving.

THE NEXT GENERATION CHALLENGE

1. Look back at the list of leadership environments in this chapter and begin jotting down the names of people whom you would trust to observe and critique you.

2. Does it scare you to be that vulnerable? If so, why?

3. What do you have to lose by engaging a leadership coach? What do you have to gain?

4. Do you have a propensity to do an end run around authority you disagree with?

5. If you can't find someone who is farther down the road of leadership to coach you, gather a group of peers and work through leadership literature together.

CHARACTER

CHARACTER DETERMINES THE
LEADER'S LEGACY

Chapter Thirteen

A NONESSENTIAL

We set young leaders up for
a fall if we encourage them to envision
what they can do before they consider
the kind of person they should be.

[R. Ruth Barton]

Let's begin this final section with a reality check: Character is not essential to leadership.

We all know of leaders who have led large organizations and garnered the loyalty of many followers, and yet lacked character. They demonstrated courage and competency. They were clear in their directives. They may have even sought the advice of others. But they were not men and women who were known for doing what was right. It is not uncommon to hear accomplished leaders attribute their success to business practices and personal conduct that most people would consider reprehensible. And yet there they are, king or queen of the mountain…at least for the moment.

As we discussed earlier, you can lead without character. *But character is what makes you a leader worth following.* Integrity is not necessary if your aspirations as a leader end with simply persuading people to follow you. But if at the end of the day your intent is for those who follow to respect you, integrity is a must. Your accomplishments as a leader will make your name known. Your character will determine what people associate with your name.

Your gifts and determination may dictate your potential, but it is your character that will determine your legacy. You can create an enviable lifestyle by leveraging your leadership skills alone. But you cannot create an enviable life without giving serious attention to who you are on the inside.

Authors James Kouzes and Barry Posner surveyed nearly 1,500 managers from around the country as part of a study sponsored by the American Management Association. They asked the following open-ended question: "What values, personal traits, or characteristics do you look for and admire in your superiors?" In other words, what makes a leader worth following?

More than 225 values, traits, and characteristics were identified. These were then reduced to fifteen categories. What these managers said they wanted most from their leaders was integrity. The categories that scored the highest marks were "integrity," "is truthful," "is trustworthy," "has character," and "has convictions."[26]

In a subsequent study they elaborated on several categories and added a few new characteristics not included in the previous study. In a two-year series of executive seminars conducted at Santa Clara University and several corporate locations, more than 2,600 top-level managers completed a checklist of superior leadership characteristics. The number-one characteristic they looked for in a leader was honesty. Honesty ranked ahead of "competency," "intelligence," and "is inspiring."[27]

These findings are supported by a study conducted jointly by Korn/Ferry International and Columbia Graduate School of business. Surveying more than 1,500 top executives in twenty countries, the study looked into strategies for growth, areas of expertise, and personal characteristics of the ideal CEO. "Ethics" was rated most highly among the personal characteristics needed by a CEO. In short, they expected their leaders to be above reproach.[28]

Those who choose to follow you want you to be a leader worth following. They will judge you not so much for where you led them, but how you led them. Their stories will always include their personal estimation of you as a person, not just your leadership skills. The truth is that those who choose to follow you will expect more from you by way of character than they expect from themselves.

Years ago I adopted a definition of character that is simple enough for me to remember yet complete enough to have teeth: *Character is the will to do what's right even when it's hard.*

Character is about *will* because it requires a willingness to make tough decisions—decisions that sometimes run contrary to emotion, intuition, economics, current trends, and in the eyes of some, common sense. Having the will to do what's right requires that you determine what's right before the struggle to do what's right ensues. Leading with character necessitates a series of predecisions. As a next generation leader you must decide ahead of time what is nonnegotiable as it relates to right and wrong.

When we talk about the will to do what's *right,* we are assuming the existence of a standard of right and wrong that

exists apart from us, an unmoving bar by which we are mea-
sured. Leaders worth following acknowledge an absolute
standard of right and wrong, one that exists independent of
their emotions, experiences, or desires. They lead with the
assumption that there is a benchmark by which all decisions
are judged.

Granted, it is not popular to speak in terms of absolutes.
But as C. S. Lewis asserted:

> Whenever you find a man who says he doesn't
> believe in real right or wrong, you will find the same
> man going back on this a moment later. He may
> break his promise to you, but if you try breaking
> one to him he'll be complaining "It's not fair" before
> you can say Jack Robinson.[29]

Character involves doing what's right because it's the
right thing to do—regardless of the cost. And it's those last
few words that divide the men and women of character
from those with good but negotiable intentions.

The most direct path to where you want to be is not
the most ethical one. How do I know that about you?
After all, we have never met! I will be the first to admit
that it is unfair for me to judge your situation without
knowing anything about it. But my hunch is that if you
were to draw a straight line from where you are to
where you want to be, and then follow it, you would be
forced to compromise morally or ethically. Somewhere
between you and your goal as a next generation leader is
a minefield.

Leaders committed to maintaining their character will often say no to what many would perceive to be the opportunity of a lifetime. The willingness to say no is what sets the leader with character apart from the pack.

The day will come when progress seems to call for a compromise of conviction. The leader in you will want to push forward. After all, you've come so far. The end certainly justifies the means. In that moment the significance of the goal will far outweigh the significance of the compromise.

But there will be another voice as well. The message will be simple, short, and without explanation: "This is wrong." Against that still, small voice you will hurl one thousand reasons, explanations, rationalizations, and illustrations. But when you are finished, the undaunted voice inside you will continue to whisper, "It's not right."

As you will discover, if you haven't already, the shortest distance between where you are and where you want to be is not the most honorable one.

The good news is that in most cases there are other paths you can take. But they are generally longer, steeper, and more expensive. Nobody likes to detour. Especially leaders. But what hangs in the balance of those inevitable dilemmas is worth the delay.

The irony of being a leader with character is that your willingness to do what is right may jeopardize your forward motion. Leading and being the person you want to be don't always line up. But it is in those moments that you discover a great deal about yourself. You discover what you value most.

Predeciding to do what's right will cost you. It will cost you time, money, and opportunity. It may negatively impact your reputation…at least for the short term. It may actually be an obstacle on your career path.

As a next generation leader you may be tempted to believe that once you attain a certain level of success, these kinds of dilemmas will dissipate. If you think this, you are mistaken. Success doesn't make anything of consequence easier. Success just raises the stakes. Success brings with it the unanticipated pressure of maintaining success. The more successful you are as a leader, the more difficult this becomes. There is far more pressure at the top of an organization than you might imagine.

If you are so fortunate as to gain success in the eyes of the public or within your organization, you will wake up one day to the realization that what was once applauded as exceptional is now expected. It is more exciting to win the world heavyweight championship than it is to defend it. It is more exhilarating to break a standing sales record than it is to try to match it year after year.

It is on the mountaintop that leaders often abandon the convictions and humility that got them there. Once they have "arrived" they are tempted to opt for a maintenance strategy that calls for an entirely different set of tools. Whether it is business, politics, or religion, the pressure to compromise in order to maintain one's success is a constant.

I have a good friend who took his company public several years ago. Up until that time he was committed to being known in his industry as a man of impeccable integrity. His charismatic personality combined with his unwavering character was infectious. Within a relatively short time he was able to find the venture capital he needed to launch what became something of an overnight success in the print industry. Throughout the process he was careful not to take shortcuts morally or ethically.

But as he made his way up the last incline, with the top of the mountain in sight, something changed. The influx of money brought on by the IPO combined with the pressure of greedy stockholders began to take its toll on him. Fear choked the life out of his vision. His quest for progress seemed to be replaced by an irrational dread of losing what he had acquired. He became defensive. Eventually he began taking medication to ease his anxiety. Throughout this ordeal he was quick to give God credit for his past success. But he began to have a difficult time trusting God to help him maintain the success he'd been given.

I believe this man has compromised his character on more than one occasion for the sake of maintaining his business success. When I have questioned him about it, he just shakes his head and says, "Andy, you don't understand." But his condescending tone betrays him. He is the one who is confused, not me. When I press him for more information, his convoluted explanations confirm my suspicion: I think he knows he is wrong. But this is the path he has chosen for now, a path that will continue to lead him away from the things he once valued most.

It is not just a leader's fear of losing his spot on the top of the mountain that sets him up for compromise. With success comes a propensity to see oneself as the final authority as it relates to right and wrong. It is not uncommon to find successful leaders playing by a different set of rules. Everything really does look different when you are at the top.

Power, money, success, fame…they are all intoxicants. And intoxicated people see the world differently. For the intoxicated leader, rules are for the common man. Not for him. What was once unthinkable becomes necessary in light of what's at stake. What was once considered dishonest is seen as prudent in light of current reality. When questioned, his response is something along the lines of, "One day you will understand."

Maybe you read a paragraph like that and think to yourself, *Not me. I'll be different.* Perhaps you will be one of the few who is able to carry the weight of success without bending to the pressure that comes with it. Or perhaps when that day arrives, you will consider your current outlook on life naïve and you'll find yourself considering options you'd always ruled out. Time will tell.

Either way, the temptation will be there to rewrite the rules.

What if you knew you could break the rules, change the rules, or even ignore the rules and get away with it? What if you knew there would never be any consequences financially or physically? Then what would you do?

Leading with character is not about doing right to avoid consequences. Leaders worth following do the right thing because it is the right thing. Virtue is not a means to an end. It is the end.

Leaders worth following don't make the rules. They lead within the guidelines that have been established before they ever came onto the scene. They recognize and submit to what is right as right has been defined by God in the hearts of men. Leaders worth following acknowledge that their leadership skills and successes never give them the right to replace what God has put in place.

Right and wrong are not determined by economic and organizational progress. They stand apart from both. At times they stand in the way of both. It is not until right and wrong impede forward motion that you discover if you are a leader worth following.

So why cling tenaciously to something that has the potential to slow you down? If leadership for the sake of personal advancement is all you are after, then there is no compelling reason. But if you desire to be a leader worth following, you really have no choice.

Here's why: What hangs in the balance of your decision to choose the way of character versus expedience is something far more valuable to you as a leader than progress. What hangs in the balance is your *moral authority*.

Every leader wears two badges: one visible, one invisible. The visible badge is your position and title. The invisible badge is your moral authority.

Your position gives you authority within a certain context, i.e., the office. Your moral authority, however, gives you influence in a variety of contexts. Your position will prompt people in your organization to lend you their hands on a temporary basis. But your moral authority will inspire them to lend you their hearts.

Moral authority is established once it becomes clear to those who are watching that progress, financial reward, and recognition are not a leader's gods. When they see that, as much as you value those things, there is something you value more, something you refuse to sacrifice at the altar of "success," you will have moral authority in their eyes.

Moral authority is the credibility you earn by walking your talk. It is the relationship other people see between what you claim to be and what you really are. It is achieved when there is perceived alignment between conviction, action, belief, and behavior. Alignment between belief and behavior makes a leader persuasive.

The invisible badge of moral authority bestows upon the leader something that money *can* buy, but only temporarily. With moral authority comes influence. And it is far easier to lead from the vantage point of influence than position alone. You can manage people without moral authority. But you cannot influence them.

We will not allow ourselves to be influenced by men and women who lack moral authority. Inconsistency between what is said and done inflicts a mortal wound on a leader's influence. Consequently, that same inconsistency hampers a leader's ability to lead.

John Maxwell was right when he said that people have to buy into the leader before they will buy into the vision. It is your moral authority that opens the door for the people around you to buy into your vision. You can pay people to work for you based on your position alone, but you cannot involve people in a cause or a movement without moral authority.

Consequently, every decision you make will either add to or detract from the influence you have with those who have chosen to follow you—even those decisions that are not directly related to your profession.

Leaders worth following do not pretend to live in two worlds. There is no discrepancy between their professional and private lives. They know the futility of compartmentalizing their lives.

You can tell yourself all day that how you conduct your life away from the office is nobody's business. Perhaps you are right. But do not be deceived: If there is a perceived difference between what you expect from others and what you expect from yourself, it will eventually erode your influence.

As a pastor who grew up in a pastor's home I know this all too well. Every time I take my family to a restaurant people have an opportunity to see whether or not I really live what I preach. How realistic is it to think that people can see me act one way in public and yet espouse a totally different standard on Sunday morning and maintain their respect for me as a leader? I may successfully compartmentalize my life, but they won't be able to.

Your situation is no different. To be a leader worth following there must be alignment between the values you preach to your organization and the values you live out in every facet of your life. If you require honesty from those you work with, then honesty must be a trait that characterizes you in all your roles.

Your position in the company may be secure, but your influence and moral authority will remain fragile. We are always one decision, one word, one reaction away from damaging what has taken years to develop.

Chapter Fourteen

THE KING WHO FOLLOWED

Character is not made in crisis;
it is only exhibited.

Everyone loves a story about a hero or heroine who chooses to stand alone against injustice. It is a theme that permeates our literature. It is why I have watched *The Patriot* at least two dozen times. It is why my kids have worn out my *Star Wars* videos. And it is this forceful theme that compelled Sandra to finally admit that *Gladiator* really was a good movie after all.

When we hear of men and women doing the right thing at the risk of losing what's most precious to them, something happens in our hearts. Not only do we want them to win in the end; we want to know that, if faced with the same dilemma, we would follow their example.

Doing the right thing when it costs something is the essence of true heroism. It is also the mark of a great leader. When you find a man or woman who will do what's right regardless of what it costs personally, you have discovered a leader worth following. When you choose to take a stand for what is right at the risk of losing what is precious to you, then you too have become a leader worth following.

My favorite Old Testament example of this principle is the story of Shadrach, Meshach, and Abednego. I love this story because these three Jewish boys had every reason to compromise their convictions, to do the wrong thing.

In 605 B.C. the armies of the Babylonian empire laid siege against the city of Jerusalem. When the city fell, the Babylonians, in their customary fashion, rounded up the brightest and best among the citizens and royalty of Jerusalem and marched them off to their capital city.

Four of those taken were Daniel, Shadrach, Meshach, and Abednego. They entered Babylon as slaves. But over time, by the providence of God, the Babylonians came to recognize that these four Jewish boys were extraordinarily gifted leaders and administrators. Consequently, they were granted places of prominence in the empire. Shadrach, Meshach and Abednego were promoted to the equivalent of city managers in Babylon. They had access to the king. All their needs were taken care of. They were set for life. They had absolutely nothing to gain by challenging their new king.

In addition to native Babylonians, the city of Babylon was inhabited by scores of people from the surrounding regions. King Nebuchadnezzar's intent was to transition these foreigners away from their native language and culture and indoctrinate them in the ways of the Babylonians.

In the book of Daniel we discover that as part of his grand strategy, King Nebuchadnezzar erected an image of gold outside the city and then ordered everyone, regardless of his previous religious affiliation, to bow and worship the image whenever certain music was played in the kingdom.[30] This was an attempt to consolidate his power and ensure that his foreign "guests" saw him and his gods as their ultimate authority. By bowing to the image, an individual was acknowledging that Nebuchadnezzar was the supreme authority and was in control of the outcome of their lives.

When Shadrach, Meshach, and Abednego heard the king's edict, they decided not to play along. Their ultimate allegiance was to their invisible King, not King Nebuchadnezzar.

When the king was made aware of their impertinence, he called them in. This is a significant detail in the story. The fact that he wanted to see them face-to-face rather than having them immediately disposed of is evidence of his unique relationship with these young men as well as their importance to his administration. These were not just three more throw-away slaves. To lose them would be a loss Nebuchadnezzar did not want to deal with unnecessarily. So he gave them a second chance to obey.

During their exchange, King Nebuchadnezzar repeated his edict and the penalty for those who disobeyed. His words echo the claims and threats that every leader faces when his character is on the line: "But if you do not worship it, you will be thrown immediately into a blazing furnace. Then what god will be able to rescue you from my hand?" (Daniel 3:15, NIV).

Nebuchadnezzar claimed to have control over the outcome of events. "You will be thrown into the blazing furnace," he declared. Translated: "I control your destiny. To maintain your current position is pointless. Futile. You have no choice but to bow."

So it is with each of us at some point along the leadership journey. Someone or some set of circumstances will stand between us and our destination. Unless we agree to temporarily abandon our integrity, all forward motion will come to a screeching halt. And as we contemplate our future and the choices that lie before us, the visible king whispers in our ear, "Then what god will be able to rescue you from my hand?"

- Then who's going to hire you?
- Then who's going to buy your product?
- Then who's going to trust you?
- Then who's going to follow you?
- Then who's going to invest in your idea?
- Then how are you going to get back on your feet financially?
- Then how are you going to pay the bills?

In those moments it is tempting to believe that the invisible King has been outmaneuvered. Trumped. It seems we have no choice but to compromise in order to keep the dream alive, the company in the black, and the cash flow positive.

Suddenly our simplistic Sunday-school faith is not only impractical, it is impracticable. Compromising—abandoning our moral authority—seems to be the only available option.

So Shadrach, Meshach, and Abednego stood respect-fully before the visible king as he reminded them that he and he alone controlled outcomes. What god had the power to rescue them from one so great as he? And then, in an uncharacteristic burst of compassion, King Nebuchadnezzar offered them a second chance: "Now when you hear the sound of the horn, flute, zither, lyre, harp, pipes and all kinds of music, if you are ready to fall down and worship the image I made, very good" (Daniel 3:15, NIV).

But they did not need a second chance. For they would not fall victim to the sincere but misinformed claims of the visible king:

> *Shadrach, Meshach and Abed-nego replied to the king,*
> *"O Nebuchadnezzar, we do not need to give you an*
> *answer concerning this matter. If it be so, our God*
> *whom we serve is able to deliver us from the furnace of*
> *blazing fire; and He will deliver us out of your hand,*
> *O king. But even if He does not, let it be known to you,*
> *O king, that we are not going to serve your gods or*
> *worship the golden image that you have set up."*
> (Daniel 3:16–18)

Translated: "O Nebuchadnezzar, we have placed our destiny in the hands of the invisible King. The one who truly controls outcomes."

Their response infuriated the king. Scripture tells us that his attitude toward the three boys changed.[31] Apparently the king was not accustomed to anyone saying no. He was accustomed to control. The whole idea behind building the statue in the first place was to reinforce his control over those who inhabited his kingdom. How dare these three Hebrew boys defy his command!

How is it that these three teenagers, far away from home and family, had the courage to go toe-to-toe with the most powerful man in the world at that time? Where did they find the courage to do the right thing even at the price of their lives?

Shadrach, Meshach, and Abednego maintained a perspective that many leaders lose as they begin to enjoy the
rewards of their success. The three Hebrew boys never lost
sight of the source of their blessing.

Nebuchadnezzar was not the reason they had been given
prestige in the city of Babylon. He was not the reason they had
become men of influence. These were gifts and blessings from
God. So why would they abandon the principles of God in
order to maintain the blessings of God? It doesn't make
sense. Why abandon the invisible King who *controls* outcomes to serve the visible king who only *claims to control*
outcomes?

In leadership there will always be visible kings who claim
to have control over the outcome of our decisions. Within
the context of the world that we see, their claims will have
merit. The temptation to give in will be real. The seemingly
unavoidable consequences of ignoring those claims will
make compromise that much more enticing. It will be the
"prudent" and "responsible" thing to do.

These scenarios present a next generation leader with
what can become his finest hour—or perhaps his final hour.
It depends upon who or what a leader views as the source of
his success. If in the moment of decision we can remember
that our talent, our opportunities, and our passion for leadership are all given to us by God; if we can remember that
our successes are the blessings of God; then perhaps we will
remember as Shadrach, Meshach, and Abednego remembered: *One need never violate the principles of God to maintain
the blessings of God. The unseen King is able.*

As we stated earlier, it is in the midst of success that
leaders often abandon the convictions and standards that

they adhered to during the journey from anonymity. When leaders begin to enjoy the rewards of success, they often forget the source of their success. The pressure to compromise in order to maintain one's success will never go away.

It is much easier to "risk it all" when there is little at risk. But success raises the stakes. Now there is something to lose. And the visible kings of this world will claim to have control over what we lose and what we keep. Their threats are real, and the consequences of ignoring them seem unavoidable.

> Success raises the stakes. Consequently, at the first critical moment, many leaders will abandon their commitment to character. Just when they have an opportunity to really lead—to jump out in front of the pack—they choose instead to follow the masses, the men and women who confuse the rewards of success with the genuine item.

But still this truth remains: There is never a reason to violate the principles of God in order to maintain the blessing of God. There is never a reason to compromise God's standards in order to maintain God's blessings. The invisible King is able to deliver us from the coercion and threats of the visible kings. Our invisible King controls outcomes. He controls the actions of those who claim to be in control. And when we who have been called to lead place our trust in His deliverance, we establish ourselves in the minds and hearts of those who observe us as leaders worth following.

As Shadrach, Meshach, and Abednego predicted, God delivered them from Nebuchadnezzar's hand. They emerged from the furnace unharmed. As a result, Nebuchadnezzar came to the startling realization that he was not in control, after all:

> Then Nebuchadnezzar said, "Praise be to the God of Shadrach, Meshach and Abednego, who has sent his angel and rescued his servants! They trusted in him and defied the king's command and were willing to give up their lives rather than serve or worship any god except their own God...." Then the king promoted Shadrach, Meshach and Abednego in the province of Babylon. (Daniel 3:28, 30, NIV)

In refusing to compromise, they gained moral authority and influence with the king. The consistency between belief and action—conviction and behavior—was overpowering, even to a man like Nebuchadnezzar. He had never witnessed that kind of commitment to an ideal. Few people have. Think about it: Three slave boys from a conquered nation radically influenced the king. How? By refusing to bow when bowing seemed to be the only option.

There will come a time in your leadership when your character will be tested. You will have an opportunity to be the hero. The opportunity will take you by surprise. In the heat of the moment you will be unaware of all that is at stake. But if you do what's right, you will look back and see that it was a defining moment for you as a leader and as an individual.

In that moment you will learn something about yourself. You will learn something about your heavenly Father. And you will have a story to tell your children.

To be an authentic test of character, it will be a situation in which the outcome will be completely out of your control. You will simply make your choice and face the consequences. It will be a trial by fire. But it will be a fire of refinement. And on the other side you will be better for it.

I have seen this principle played out many times in the lives of friends and acquaintances. The fear of the unknown is eventually replaced by a brand of freedom reserved only for those who are willing to live with the consequences of uncompromising virtue.

If you make the right decision and choose to embrace the consequences, you will find a level of freedom that you did not know existed. You will be free from the threats of those who claim to have the power to control the outcome of your life. You will be free to say no to the kings who would abuse their authority by attempting to manipulate you. You will be free to serve the invisible King and to say no to all the would-be kings who claim authority over you.

That single event will make you a better leader. In the moment of decision you will gain insight into who you are and more importantly, whose you are.

Chapter Fifteen

THE LEADER WORTH FOLLOWING

The integrity of the upright
will guide them, but the crookedness of
the treacherous will destroy them.

[Proverbs 11:3]

Your talent and giftedness as a leader have the potential to take you farther than your character can sustain you. That ought to scare you.

The fact that people choose to follow you is not necessarily an indicator that you deserve to be followed. There is a significant difference between having a following and being worth following. The truth is that talented, charismatic, visionary people will almost always have a following. Whether they are worth following is a different question, predicated upon a different set of values.

There is always the temptation to look at someone and judge the amount of God's blessing upon his life based upon the number of people who have chosen to follow him. But if numbers tell the whole story, we would have to assume that God removed His blessing from Jesus toward the end of His ministry! In the weeks prior to His crucifixion the crowds began to wane. In the end there were only a handful of faithful men and women who dared to be associated with

Him. Followship is not an accurate indicator of one's worthiness to be followed.

To become a leader worth following, you must give time and attention to the inner man. To leave a legacy that goes beyond accomplishment alone, a leader must devote himself to matters of the heart.

There is no necessary correlation between talent and maturity. Hollywood has taught us that. For that matter, there is no correlation between talent and common sense either. We have all seen parents give their children gifts that were beyond their ability to handle. Cars, pocketknives, and cell phones all come with instruction manuals, but not maturity manuals. There is no correlation between what we can own and what we can responsibly operate.

If you have been blessed with the gift of leadership, remember it is just that—a gift. But owning the gift and operating the gift responsibly are two different things. One requires nothing on your part. The other requires a lifetime of learning. The gift is recognized over time. The maturity to use it responsibly is developed over time too. Recognizing your giftedness is unavoidable. But taking the time to develop the maturity to handle it responsibly requires initiative and discipline.

Leaders get themselves into trouble when the momentum of their giftedness propels them past their ability to sustain the pace and handle the pressures of accomplishment. Your eventual success will introduce you to new temptations, new options, and new opportunities. Your response to these depends entirely upon the condition of your heart.

As a next generation leader it is incumbent upon you to do all you can *now* to prepare yourself for your eventual success. Your gifts will open doors. Your character will determine what you do once those doors have opened.

Odds are, you are giving proper attention to the task at hand. You are counting the things that need to be counted and organizing the things that need to be organized. No doubt you have a mission statement and a set of values to support it. In time, those elements, combined with your God-given abilities, will take you far. People will follow.

But your natural talent will eventually outstrip and outpace your character if you do not develop a parallel track upon which to run. To become a leader worth following, you must be intentional about developing the inner man. You must invest in the health of your soul. Nobody plans to fail, especially leaders. But to ignore the condition of your soul is the equivalent of planning to fail.

The day will come when the wanna-be kings in your world will whisper in your ear, and you will be tempted to abandon what's right for the sake of progress, profit, or expediency. If you have neglected character, you will go to draw upon the depth of your convictions but find little there to sustain you. You may retain your position as leader. But you will have abandoned your opportunity to finish as a leader worth following.

The time to begin preparing for that eventuality is now. You can perhaps wait until the night before your real-estate final to sit down and prepare, but there is no cramming for a test of character. It always comes as a pop quiz. You're either ready or you're not. It is the law of the harvest at work. In the moment of testing you will reap what you have sown.

There are things you can do now to prepare you for that inevitable day of testing. The first is to begin at the end. The second is to make your convictions public.

BEGIN AT THE END

The best place to begin preparing is the end. Character development always begins with the end in mind. What do you want to be remembered for?

What do you want your best friend to say at your funeral? How about your children? Your spouse? What do you want your kids to tell your grandchildren about you? How would you want the people who knew you best to describe your life? In other words, what do you want to be?

I hope that as an emerging next generation leader it is becoming clearer to you what you want to accomplish, what you want to *do*. The question is: Have you determined what you want to *become?* Your doing will flow from who you are. The outer man will reflect the inner man. The inner man determines the legacy of the outer man.

Six months after Sandra and I were married, I spent a half a day working through those questions. At the time I wasn't leading any organization of significance. But it was a time when the news was filled with stories of recognized spiritual leaders failing morally and ethically. It wasn't their poor leadership decisions that had sidelined them. It was their poor personal decisions that had taken them out. The inner man hadn't kept pace with the outer man.

This exercise led me to my personal definition of success. I narrowed it down to nine words: available, accountable, dependable, generous, honest, loyal, pure, sensitive, and transparent. Those nine terms form a perimeter around my behavior. For me, dishonesty is not merely a sin. It represents failure. To say yes to speaking engagements at the expense of being available to my children is not simply misprioritization. It is failure.

As a next generation leader you need to build a moral perimeter around your behavior too. You must come to grips with the fact that, ultimately, success is defined in terms of who you are and how you treat the people around you.

To charge off in the direction of the task without first determining who you want to be and how you plan to treat those who choose to follow is tantamount to running from home plate to third base. And as my friend Kevin Myers says, the only time that's funny is in little league. In leadership, it is a shortcut that short circuits legacy.

MAKE IT PUBLIC

Once you have determined what you want to be, tell somebody. Go public with your intentions. Is it really anybody else's business? You bet it is. Character is personal, but it is not private. Everybody who knows you has an opinion about the kind of person you are. You might as well let them know the kind of person you are striving to become.

> Leaders worth following predetermine their response to invitations and opportunities that have the potential to sink them morally and ethically. While uncertainty is unavoidable in the external world of leadership, next generation leaders have no uncertainty when it comes to guarding their character.

Letting others in on who you want to be reinforces the perimeter you are staking out around your behavior. When you know that others know the value you place on something, it is powerful incentive to check any behavior that might take you out of bounds. And on those inevitable occasions when you do drift across the line, the fact that others know is incentive to take responsibility for your actions.

Years ago I informed our leadership team and our elders that I had made it a priority to leave the office every day by four-fifteen. Since I went public with my schedule, people are constantly asking me if I am still sticking by my commitment. When I have to stay late for a meeting, people in the office look at me funny and say things like, "What are you still doing here?"

I'll never forget hearing a good friend of mine share his definition of success with a large group of people. By sharing it publicly, he made himself accountable to those who are close enough to watch. It was an invitation for evaluation. This is what he said his definition of success was: "For those who know me best to love and respect me most."

It is hard to beat that. Every time I'm with him I think about that statement. And the truth is that the better I get to know him, the more I *do* love and respect him. Above and beyond his career success, here's a guy who is being successful where it matters most. And he has put himself on display.

Your character is always showing. So why not talk about it? Why not reveal the desire of your heart with a few close friends? In doing so you reinforce the strength of your perimeter. Should you drift, there will be someone there to draw it to your attention.

This came home to me in a personal way during my first job after graduate school. A major religious leader had just been exposed for a moral problem that, he later acknowledged, had begun for him in high school. People were shocked and outraged. An empire built on trust came tumbling down, and the Christian community received another black eye.

I remember where I was when I heard his public apology on the radio. That same night I was hit with this thought: *What small thing in my life right now has the potential to grow into a big thing?* And close behind it came this thought: *And who knows about it other than me?* This was the beginning of a lifestyle of accountability. I decided then that it would be better to expose my weaknesses early to a handful of people who loved me than to run the risk of being exposed publicly to people who couldn't care less.

At the time I wasn't leading anything. My decision to seek out accountability wasn't a leadership decision. But looking back, that decision has had a profound effect on my leadership.

As a next generation leader you owe it to yourself as well as to those you will someday lead to identify and resolve those baby dragons that have the potential to grow up and devour not only you, but those who will put their trust in you. Leaders who refuse to make the development of their character a priority generally end up with organizations that reflect that deficit as well.

Your character is reflected in every decision you make and every relationship you establish.

In closing, I would like to share something that has become a nightly routine at the Stanley household. It started several years ago when I would pray with Andrew at bedtime. At the end of my prayers I would say, "Lord, give Andrew the wisdom to know what's right and the courage to do what's right, even when it's hard."

Before long he assimilated that request into his bedtime prayers as well. Now every night at bedtime all five members of our family ask God to give them the wisdom to know what's right and the courage to do what's right, even when it's hard.

The day will come when each of my kids will face a defining moment. Doing the right thing will be hard. The visible kings in their lives will assure them that they really have no choice but to bow and compromise.

Perhaps in that moment of decision their invisible King will in fact give them the wisdom to know and the courage to do what is right.

TO BE AN EFFECTIVE LEADER . . .

- Understand that character is not essential to leadership, but character is what sets you apart as a leader worth following. Talent and determination determine your potential; character determines your legacy.

- Choose to do what's right, even when it is hard. The more successful you become, the harder it will be to maintain integrity. Small compromises early in the journey will make it easier to compromise on the big things later on.

- Don't fool yourself. Surviving small indiscretions deceives many leaders into thinking that they will be equally successful in surviving the bigger ones down the line. History tells us that nothing could be further from the truth.

- Never violate the principles of God to gain or maintain the blessing of God. What you gain on your own, you will be forced to protect and manage on your own.

- Remember, your character is always on display. It shapes your reactions, your attitudes, and your priorities. Likewise, your character shapes the experience of those who choose to journey with you—and therefore will determine who is left standing in your corner when the journey draws to a close.

THE NEXT GENERATION CHALLENGE

1. What is your greatest temptation? Who have you told?

2. As you think about where you are professionally versus where you want to be, what or who stands in your way?

3. In light of those obstacles, what are the shortcuts you will most likely be tempted to take?

4. What do you want to be remembered for?

5. What's your plan?

EPILOGUE

By God's divine and mysterious appointment you have been blessed with the ability to command the attention and influence the direction of others. You are a leader.

This capacity to influence and mobilize is a gift. But it is a gift that comes to you in raw form. Like music or art, leadership must be developed if it is to be used effectively. As is the case in the development of any skill or talent, you must begin with the fundamentals. The five principles I've covered in this book are the fundamentals of next generation leadership.

You must discover and play to your strengths and delegate your weaknesses. You've got to be courageous, and you've got to be clear in the midst of uncertainty. You need to find a leadership coach. And along the way it is absolutely essential that you maintain your character.

If you embrace and internalize these five essentials, you will have the foundation you need to leverage the opportunities God brings your way. Ignore any one of these five, and you will expend an inordinate measure of energy with little progress to show for it. If you have ever driven on ice, you know that horsepower is worthless without traction. These five essentials will provide you with the traction you need to maximize your leadership potential.

As you embark on your quest to shape the future, remember that in the wake of your leadership is the next crop of next generation leaders. They are easy to spot: They will remind you of you when you were their age. They will be the ones asking all the questions. They will be the influencers. In some cases, they will be the trouble-makers. But most importantly, they are your responsibility.

You can ignore them or just put up with them. Or you can do for them what others have done for you. You can give to them what others have given to you. Opportunity. Information. Encouragement. Hope.

Never forget that your legacy will not be defined merely by the organizations you lead or the products you develop. Your legacy will be reflected in the lives you influence and the leaders who follow in your footsteps. These fortunate individuals will walk for a time in the shadow of your talents and abilities. Their lives will bear your signature.

Jesus assured us that to whom much has been given, much will be required.[32] As a leader you have been given much. As a next generation leader you have been given the ability to shape the future.

For other resources by Andy Stanley, please contact:

North Point Resources
4350 North Point Parkway
Alpharetta, Georgia 30022
866-866-5621
www.northpoint.org

The publisher and author would love to hear
your comments about this book. Please contact us at:
www.multnomah.net/nextgeneration

1. John Maxwell rates a leader's effectiveness on a scale of one to ten, with a ten being the perfect leader. His observation is that tens attract eights and nines. A seven leader will attract fives and sixes. An extraordinarily secure leader may at times attract leaders who have superior leadership skills.

2. Stephen R. Covey, *The 7 Habits of Highly Effective People* (New York: Simon and Schuster, 1989), 171.

3. The church expected Christ to return at any moment. Consequently they were pooling their resources to support one another while they waited. Acts 4:35 tells us that the apostles were given the responsibility of distributing money as it was needed by those who were daily joining the ranks of the church.

4. The early church was made up primarily of Jews. There were two branches: national Jews and Hellenistic Jews. The Hellenistic Jews were Jews born outside of Israel and more Greek in their cultural orientation. These Hellenistic Jews were either recent transplants or had come to Jerusalem for Pentecost and had then decided to stay, based on their assumption that Jesus would return at any moment.

5. See Acts 8 and Acts 21:8.

6. Richard Koch, *The 80/20 Principle* (New York: Currency/Doubleday, 1998), 4.

7. The ability to distinguish between passions and core competencies is essential to your development as a leader. Sometimes we have a difficult time distinguishing between the two. There are things we love to do that we are not really very good at and never will be. I would rather play the piano than write. Like many people, I love music. But I would be foolish to dedicate my life to becoming a professional musician. It is important to

know which of our passions are not in sync with our natural abilities.

8. Covey, *The 7 Habits of Highly Effective People*, 171.

9. James M. Kouzes and Barry Z. Posner, *The Leadership Challenge* (San Francisco: Jossey-Bass, Inc., 1987), 48.

10. Max De Pree, *Leadership Jazz* (New York: Doubleday, 1992), 144.

11. Warren Bennis and Burt Nanus, *Leaders* (New York: Harper Perennial, 1985), 76.

12. First Samuel 18:6–7.

13. First Samuel 18:3–4. By giving David his cloak and weapons, Jonathan was in effect pledging his possessions and his protection to David.

14. First Samuel 18:9.

15. Mike Nappa, *The Courage to Be Christian* (West Monroe, La.: Howard Pub., 2001), 81.

16. Jim Collins, *Good to Great* (New York: HarperCollins, 2001), 139–40.

17. Al Ries, *Focus* (New York: Harper Business, 1996), 78.

18. Peter M. Senge, *The Fifth Discipline* (New York: Currency/Doubleday, 1990), 155.

19. Included in a talk given at the 2000 Catalyst Conference in Atlanta, Georgia.

20. Collins, *Good to Great*, 89.

21. Covey, *The 7 Habits of Highly Effective People*, 99.

22. Kouzes and Posner, *The Leadership Challenge*, np.

23. "Reyes, the Real Force Behind Agassi," SportsLine.com wire report (February 13, 2001, Las Vegas).

24. I want to thank my good friend, Fran Lamatina, for this valuable insight.

25. James C. Hunter, *The Servant* (Roseville, Calif.: Prima Publishing, 1998), 33.

26. Kouzes and Posner, *The Leadership Challenge*, 16.

27. Ibid., 17.
28. James M. Kouzes and Barry Z. Posner, *Credibility* (San Francisco: Jossey-Bass, Inc., 1993), 15.
29. C. S. Lewis, *The Case for Christianity* (New York: Macmillan Publishers, 1943), 5.
30. Daniel 3:1–6.
31. Daniel 3:19.
32. Luke 12:48.

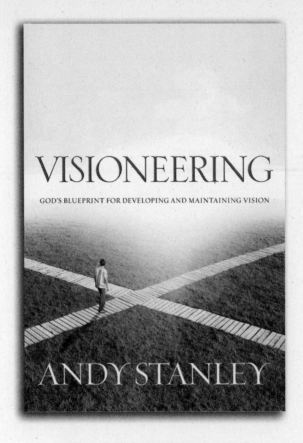

VISIONEERING

by Andy Stanley

Andy Stanley shows readers how to set goals and obliterate
the obstacles to a passionately lived, meaningful life. He
offers a workable plan for discovering a life vision aligned
with God's own vision.

ISBN 1-59052-456-X

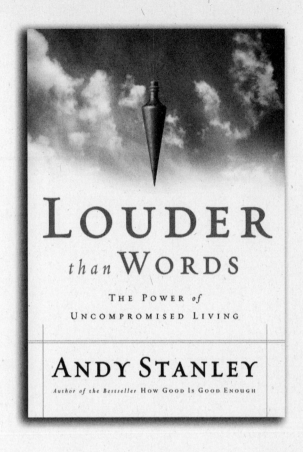

LOUDER THAN WORDS

by Andy Stanley

Sharing a strategy for personal character development, Andy Stanley helps you determine your personal definition of success and introduces a step-by-step program for prioritizing your life, overcoming barriers, and more.

ISBN 1-59052-346-6

www.mpbooks.com

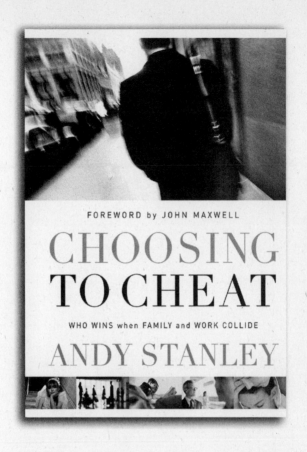

CHOOSING TO CHEAT

by Andy Stanley

This book presents a strategic plan for resolving the tension between work and home—reversing the destructive pattern of giving to your company and career what belongs to your family.

ISBN 1-59052-329-6

www.mpbooks.com

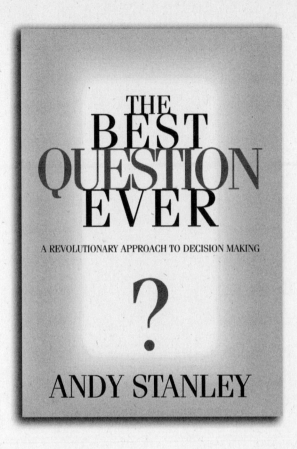

THE BEST QUESTION EVER
by Andy Stanley

When it comes to sorting out the complexities of each unique situation we face, only wisdom can reveal the best path. The question posed here will empower you to make regretless decisions every time.

ISBN 1-59052-390-3